NOT THE FUTURE WE ORDERED

NOT THE FUTURE WE ORDERED

Peak Oil, Psychology, and the Myth of Progress

John Michael Greer

KARNAC

First published in 2013 by
Karnac Books
118 Finchley Road
London NW3 5HT

British Library Cataloguing in Publication Data

A C.I.P. card for this book is available from the British Library

ISBN: 978–1–78049–088–5

Edited, designed, and produced by Communication Crafts

www.karnacbooks.com

CONTENTS

NOT THE FUTURE WE ORDERED

ONE
The unmentionable crisis

It is a curious and recurring reality in social history that the crises that come to define entire eras are very often those that, until they burst into the forefront of public attention, no one affected by them was willing to discuss at all. Betty Friedan's cogent description of depression and anomie among post-war American women as "the problem that has no name" (Friedan, 1963) could have been applied with equal justice to the symptoms of other imminent crises—for example, the social costs of slavery in the antebellum South. In these and many other cases, a reality that would shortly become the focus of explosive controversy and dramatic social change remained unmentioned and unmentionable among those who were in the closest contact with it.

Central to the process of inattention that kept these issues out of the sphere of public discussion was an act of reframing that transformed a collective crisis into an individual pathology. Physicians in the slave states before the Civil War, for example, argued that people of African origin suffered from a peculiar mental illness called "drapetomania", an irrational compulsion to run away from home. This convenient theory allowed the efforts of slaves to escape to freedom in the North to be understood, not as a response to the unmentionable social realities of slavery, but, rather, as a personal pathology that could be discussed and treated without reference to its collective context.

In the same way, the women Betty Friedan interviewed in her research by and large identified the collapse of meaning and value in their lives as a personal problem rather than a reflection of dysfunctional social realities. In this assessment, they were supported by a galaxy of authority figures, mostly male, for whom any sign of mismatch between a woman and her social setting inevitably reflected the psychological or moral inadequacies of the woman. Drapetomania thus had its precise equivalent in "housewife syndrome", a hard-to-define neurotic condition that was generally treated with daily doses of tranquilizers such as Newtown. Here again, symptoms of a collective crisis were reframed as the problems of individuals, so that any discussion of the crisis and its implications for the broader social setting could be put off as long as possible. Psychiatrists, physicians, and other members of the helping professions of the time who accepted this reframing—as most did—became unwitting enablers of the act of collective inattention that was creating the problems they thought they were treating.

A similar reframing of collective problems as individual inadequacy, driven by a similar unwillingness to face a pervasive but unmentionable social reality, plays a massive role in today's industrial societies. Throughout Europe, North America, and the developed nations of East Asia, hundreds of millions of people who grew up expecting steady improvement in standards of living, upward mobility, and a social safety net to protect them against the threat of poverty find themselves struggling to cope with an economic and political reality that more and more often fails to provide these things. Year after year, more former workers join the ranks of the permanently jobless; outside the narrowing circle of the very rich, wages and benefits shrink; costs of energy, food, and other necessities ratchet upwards; governments struggle to pay for public services that were amply funded ten or twenty years ago. Such markers of systemic crisis are everywhere, but very few people are willing to take the risk of addressing them as symptoms of a collective reality.

Instead, these problems are redefined in personal terms, as a lack of appropriate skills or sufficient motivation on the part of individuals. The political sphere is particularly committed to redefinitions of this sort. In America today, for example, one set of politicians promotes job training as a cure-all for unemployment, as though training people for jobs that do not exist will make those jobs magically appear. Another set of politicians insists that those who fall behind in the struggle to stay out of poverty are wholly responsible for their own condition. Right-wing media personality Neal Boortz, arguing along these latter lines, has gone so far as to invent a precise current equivalent of drapetomania and "housewife syndrome" by insisting that poverty is a mental disease (Boortz, 2007).

The redefinition of collective crisis in personal terms takes another, equally unhelpful form among those who see the current troubles of industrial society as the result of deliberate malignity on someone's part. Searching for scapegoats is a common habit in troubled times, especially when the source of the trouble is either unknown or unmentionable, and that habit has accordingly seen plenty of exercise in recent years. Bankers, speculators, immigrants, Muslims, Jews, labour unions, the selfish rich, the welfare-dependent poor, politicians of the left, politicians of the right—there is no shortage of candidates for blame, and the fact that some members of each of these categories (and every other category of human beings, of course) behave from time to time in some reprehensible fashion or other simply feeds the counterproductive but deeply human desire to put a face upon the otherwise faceless experience of crisis.

A constellation of potent psychological needs rooted in the subjective experience of powerlessness makes this personalization of collective crisis difficult to resist. To insist that the jobless could find jobs if only they got the right training, or that the poor would not be poor if they would simply work harder and save more, is to insist that human agency trumps the realities of a contracting economy. To insist that a troubled economy is troubled only because of the misdeeds of greedy speculators, corrupt governments, or some other scapegoat *du jour* is equally an affirmation of agency, since it implies that changes in economic conditions occur only in obedience to the will of certain human beings. The belief that the economy might be directed by a malevolent Other, appalling though that suggestion may seem to be, is arguably easier to face than the possibility that important features of economic life are not subject to human control—that, in effect, nobody is in charge at all.

Still, there is more going on in the current situation than this, just as there was more to the evasions surrounding the condition of women in 1950s America or the condition of slaves in the antebellum South. In both these latter cases, evasion of the collective and inescapable nature of crisis was driven by the collision between an emotionally powerful and widely accepted cultural narrative and a set of intrusive realities that failed to conform to it. In 1950s America, the narrative claimed that women naturally found their personal fulfilment in a set of social roles that valued them only as a support system for husbands and children. In the antebellum South, the narrative claimed that people of African descent were contented with their lot as slaves and were unfit for any other role in American society. In both cases, the gap between the narrative and the everyday realities of experience in the society that the narrative sought to justify turned into a fault line along which tectonic social changes eventually took place.

Today's industrial world faces a similar gap between a compelling cultural narrative used to justify core elements of modern society, on the one hand, and a universe that shows no interest in conforming to the narrative's core assertions, on the other. That gap is becoming a central social fact of our time, and its widening impact on individual lives and relationships makes it a psychological fact as well, one that deserves close attention from members of the helping professions as well as students of social psychology.

The cultural narrative in question is the belief in progress, which in our age has provided the normative vision of the shape of humanity's future The inconvenient realities with which that narrative fails to deal are a collection of hard physical and geological limits to the perpetual economic and technological growth central to most iterations of the belief in progress, and, in particular, one such limit: the phenomenon of peak oil. The nature of the narrative, the facts that refuse to fit it, and the likely impacts of the conflict between them on society and individuals alike—these are the central themes of this book.

HUBBERT'S CURVE

To begin exploring the gap between narrative and reality central to our society's current predicament, it will be helpful to start with an otherwise unremarkable meeting of the American Petroleum Institute in San Antonio, Texas, in 1956. At that meeting, Marion King Hubbert, a geologist then employed by Shell Oil, presented a paper announcing that petroleum production in the United States would peak and go into permanent decline around 1970 (Hubbert, 1956).

The context of that paper needs to be recalled. In the 1950s, the United States produced more oil annually than any other nation on earth—at some points during that decade, more than every other nation on earth put together. The American oil industry had immense petroleum reserves that had already been found, and it also had the world's most advanced and innovative technologies for finding new reserves. Oil could be discovered and produced so easily that the federal government quietly tolerated a technically illegal price-fixing scheme, managed by the Texas Railroad Commission, that set production limits on American oil companies to keep the price of oil from crashing to ruinously low levels. The idea that geological limits might restrict US oil production in the relatively near future seemed absurd enough that Hubbert's superiors at Shell Oil tried to talk him out of presenting his findings to the conference.

Still, Hubbert was not a man who backed down easily. He had already earned a reputation as one of the most innovative petroleum geologists of his time, and he had developed a variety of important mathematical models still much used in the oil industry, particularly the Hubbert curve, which accurately anticipates the lifetime yield of an oil well from its first few months of production. By the time he began work on the 1956 paper, he had already shown that similar calculations could be applied just as successfully to the output of an oilfield, forecasting the production of wells not yet drilled from the yield of the first few wells. His presentation to the American Petroleum Institute meeting applied the same logic to work up a rough estimate for the future production curve for the entire United States. The exact volume of oil that would eventually be produced was less important than the central point he hoped to make, which was that oil production on any scale—from a well, a field, or a country—rises, peaks, and falls over time, for reasons that are rooted in the geology of petroleum itself.

It is important to understand the logic behind Hubbert's prediction, partly because that logic will play a central role in defining the future that all of us will shortly inhabit, and partly because most of the arguments currently being used to dismiss the implications of Hubbert's work begin by misstating the reasoning that underlies it. The starting point for the Hubbert curve is the simple fact that petroleum in the ground is found in pores in permeable rocks and can only move through those rocks so fast. The details differ from one oilfield to another, depending on a galaxy of factors, but for every well there is an optimum rate at which oil can be extracted from the ground; exceeding that rate causes a larger fraction of the total oil in place to stay trapped in the rock, and so buys short-term gains at the cost of long-term losses. Thus, the lifetime production curve from a competently managed oil well resembles a plateau with one steep side and one sloping side: production rises rapidly from a starting point of zero to the optimum, stays there for a period of months or years, and then tapers off gradually to zero as the well runs dry.

The lifetime production curve of an oilfield is the sum of the production curves of all the wells in that field, which are spread out over the time needed to locate and drill more wells once the first, exploratory well strikes oil. In practice, though the mathematics are somewhat different, the curve closely resembles the bell-shaped curve beloved of statisticians. The lifetime production curve of what petroleum geologists call an oil province—a region in which the same broad geological patterns produce a series of similar oilfields—follows a similar pattern. Thus, oil provinces as well as oilfields see production gradually rise to a rounded peak or plateau and then just as gradually decline to zero.

Hubbert's 1956 paper took the same principle one step further and offered a prediction of the petroleum production curve for the United States as a whole. Production rates nationwide since the drilling of the first American oil well at Titusville, Pennsylvania, in 1859 had followed the same trajectory as oil production from a single oilfield or oil province; Hubbert simply applied his calculations to that curve to find the approximate date at which US petroleum production would reach its peak levels and begin moving towards permanent decline. That date, his paper argued, would almost certainly fall between 1968 and 1972.

To say that this prediction was not well received is to understate the case considerably. Most petroleum geologists at the time dismissed Hubbert's prediction as an exercise in needless pessimism, and very few people outside the petroleum industry paid any attention to it at all. The United States continued building freeways and suburbs, secure in the belief that there would always be enough oil to fuel lifestyles that consumed more petroleum and other fossil fuels with every passing year. That belief remained welded into place in the American psyche right up until 1970, when Hubbert's prediction came true.

The peak of US petroleum production in that year dealt a staggering blow to a nation that had convinced itself that its future would lead nowhere but up. The extraordinary prosperity of the United States in the decades following the Second World War had many causes, but the direct and indirect impacts of the torrent of black gold that flowed out of wells in Pennsylvania, Texas, Oklahoma, California, and a half dozen other states played a huge role in making that boomtime possible, in much the same way that the huge coal deposits of the Appalachians and Britain's coal belt had driven an earlier age of industrial prosperity.

After 1970, to be sure, the oil kept flowing. Frantic efforts to expand production were an obvious response; new wells were drilled in existing oil provinces, new oilfields and oil provinces were found and brought into production, and environmental concerns were elbowed aside to make way for a pipeline across Alaska so that oil from the remote North Slope fields could reach an ice-free port. None of these measures brought US petroleum production up past its 1970 peak, but the deficit could be made up by importing more oil from abroad, especially from the booming petrostates of the Persian Gulf. The difficulty was not that the United States was running out of oil; it was simply that an economy geared to constant growth in energy consumption now had to pay foreign suppliers for an ever-increasing share of its fuel supply, at prices that could no longer be regulated by the Texas Railroad Commission. That was enough to tip the United

States into a decade of economic stagnation, soaring prices, and political turmoil.

In 1972, as the first hard consequences of the US petroleum peak were just beginning to hit, Hubbert took his analysis the next step and gave testimony to a Senate committee projecting the peak of petroleum production for the entire world (Hubbert, 1974). This was a far more difficult project, since his methods depended on accurate figures for production and estimated reserves from the oilfields and oil provinces in question. These were readily available for the United States, but many other countries—notably Russia and the nations of the Persian Gulf—treated information of this kind as state secrets, and indeed still do. Rough guesses based on limited knowledge of regional geology had to serve instead. On that tentative basis, he suggested that the worldwide peak of petroleum production would likely take place sometime around the year 2000.

That prediction, reworked in various ways for public consumption and often restated in much more simplistic terms, became a central concern of the alternative energy movement and the broader counterculture scene during the decade that followed its publication. The petrol queues and soaring energy costs of the 1970s provided an immediate incentive to conservation and a variety of new energy technologies, but behind these short-term factors also lay a recognition, remarkably widespread during that decade, that remaining dependent on steadily depleting petroleum supplies was a fool's game in the long run. A great many books on energy and the environment published during that decade thus referenced Hubbert's prediction as evidence that something more than temporary fixes would be needed to ensure the survival of industrial civilization (e.g., Ehrlich, Ehrlich, & Holdren, 1977).

THE ROAD NOT TAKEN

These warnings did not fail to have an effect. The decade of the 1970s also marked the emergence of environmental concerns as a significant force in most of the world's industrial nations, as the ecological costs of the post-war boom became too obvious to ignore. The twin challenges of resource depletion and environmental pollution inspired a great many efforts to find lifeways that were less dependent on the consumption of non-renewable resources and the production of toxic pollutants, and a certain idealism left over from the movements of the 1960s inspired hopes that the industrial world might successfully reinvent itself, find some way around the implications of Hubbert's prediction, and build new societies that could provide many of the benefits of industrialism to the world's population without the vulnerabilities to depletion and the long-term environmental costs that came with fossil fuels.

Central to any such project was the challenge of finding replacements for petroleum and the other fossil fuels, which provided (and still provide) the vast majority of energy used in the world's industrial nations. Petroleum was always the biggest part of that challenge, since it provides the single largest share—some 40%—of energy used worldwide, including nearly all transportation fuel and nearly all the energy used to extract other energy resources. Still, it was widely recognized at the time that all the fossil fuels, as well as fissionable uranium, were non-renewable resources subject to curves similar to Hubbert's and that all would have to be replaced or abandoned in due time.

During the 1970s, most of the energy options now under discussion were tested, and nearly all of them proved to be unworkable. By the end of the decade, two possibilities remained, and public debate concerning energy futures had come to focus almost exclusively on the choice between them.

The first of these options proposed a near-total rebuilding of industrial society, centred on a smorgasbord of conservation and efficiency measures that would allow the world to get by on a fraction of its then-current energy requirements. That decrease in demand would make it possible, in turn, for remaining energy needs to be met from such abundant but diffuse natural energy sources as sun and wind. The decade of the 1970s saw a great deal of technical innovation along these lines (e.g., deMoll, 1977; Todd & Todd, 1980), as well as parallel explorations of the lifestyle changes that would be needed to cope with a world of sharply limited energy supplies (e.g., Callenbach, 1975; Johnson, 1978).

The other option rejected any idea of decreasing energy use and turned, instead, to nuclear power as the only way to keep energy supplies expanding at what was then their current rate of growth. A rapid buildout of nuclear power plants was the first stage of that project, but it was widely recognized that sharp geological limits on the world's supply of fissionable uranium made that only a temporary measure. Over the longer term, the nuclear option depended on massive investments in research into breeder reactor and fusion power technologies, in the hope that one or the other could be brought on line soon enough to provide long-term energy supplies for the industrial world before the remaining fuel for conventional reactors ran out.

Both these proposals involved significant risks, drastic potential downsides, and very considerable price tags. Both also required people throughout the industrial world to accept sharp limits on energy and prosperity in their own lives in order to achieve a better future for their grandchildren.

Despite these drawbacks, most informed opinion by the end of the 1970s assumed that one or the other option would define the shape of the energy future for the industrial world, and lively debates between the proponents of the two plans could be heard in popular as well as technical literature during those years. What no one apparently anticipated at the time was that a third option would be chosen instead.

That option came into play by way of the Thatcher–Reagan counterrevolution. In the United States, Britain, and several other countries factions in each of the main conservative parties gambled that they could win elections by insisting that resource depletion, pollution, and the other concerns of the "green decade" of the 1970s simply didn't matter, and that market forces would take care of any difficulties with energy supplies and ecological damage. That gamble paid off spectacularly at the polls, as voters turned with evident relief to politicians who insisted that sacrifices weren't needed and everything would turn out for the best.

It paid off even more spectacularly in the economic sphere, as the governments that swept into power on this basis shifted the exploitation of oilfields in the North Sea and Alaska North Slope into overdrive. Earlier plans had envisioned eking out these new oilfields over many decades, to cushion the transition to less abundant and concentrated energy resources. Instead, under Thatcher and Reagan and their respective successors, the new fields were pumped as fast as their geology would allow, in order to flood the market with oil, drive down prices, and generate short-term prosperity with no regard for the long-term consequences.

In the wake of the 1970s oil shortages, conservation measures had already forced down world petroleum consumption by some 15%, and this drop in demand combined with the surge in production from the North Slope and North Sea sent the price of oil plummeting. By the middle of the 1980s, that price settled in the neighbourhood of $10 a barrel—adjusted for inflation, the lowest price in recorded history—and stayed there for well over a decade. The difficult years of the 1970s and early 1980s gave way to a boom lavish enough to pay for as much imported oil as the industrial world's middle classes could consume. Hubbert's curve and the troubling predictions based on it dropped out of the consciousness of the time so completely that standard reference works on energy written after the early 1980s routinely failed to note that petroleum production would peak and decline long before the world's last oil wells ran dry (e.g., Ramage, 1997).

None of these changes affected the reality of the industrial world's dependence on fossil fuels, and on petroleum in particular. They simply made it possible to ignore that dependence for a few decades longer, and thus allowed the industrial world to back itself into a corner from which there would be few palatable escapes. It is one of the bitter ironies of recent history that the few decades of wilful blindness bought by the political manoeuvrings of the early 1980s comprised exactly the window of time that would have been needed to make a successful transition from fossil fuels to some more enduring energy source.

The Hirsch Report, a study commissioned by the US Department of Energy and released in 2005, showed that preparations for a peak in global oil production would have to be started at least twenty years in advance of the peak to avoid severe economic and social disruptions (Hirsch, Bezdek, & Wendling, 2005). In 1980, those twenty years were still available, and the hard work of the previous decade had established many of the foundations for a transition to a more energy-efficient society powered by renewable energy sources. The abandonment of those promising first steps in the early 1980s foreclosed that option. Once that choice was made, the industrial world was committed to a trajectory that, if Hubbert's prediction turned out to be correct, was guaranteed not to end well.

In the boom times of the 1980s and 1990s, very few people were even willing to think about that possibility, and no one in public life admitted taking it seriously. Still, it is telling that the same years that saw the collapse of the movement towards sustainability also witnessed a dramatic shift in cultural mood across the industrial world, as the relative optimism and idealism of the 1970s gave way, over a very short time, to a pervasive cynicism and a loudly expressed contempt for the very ideals that so many people had so recently claimed to value. An era that watched *The Waltons* and listened to John Denver's music was abruptly replaced by one that idolized "material girl" Madonna and made a mantra of Gordon Gekko's catchphrase "Greed is good". Such shifts make a useful barometer of the collective conscience of a society, and the sullen and jeering tone with which so many people dismissed the hopes they themselves had embraced not so long ago may indicate that a great many of those people recognized, on some level, that they had given themselves temporary prosperity at the cost of cashing in on their ideals, along with any hope of a liveable future for their descendants.

Whatever the sources of the troubled collective conscience that these shifts suggest, public attention to the state of the world's petroleum reserves was not among them. The world's consumption of petroleum products climbed to all-time highs as SUVs rolled off the assembly lines and a newly globalized economy shipped products around the planet, but no one in government or business paid the least attention to the possibility that Hubbert's second prediction might turn out to be as correct as his first. That lack of attention continued even after the unthinkable happened and the prediction came true.

PEAK OIL

The first signs of renewed trouble surfaced in the late 1990s, as oil industry analysts began to take stock of the fact that the rate of discovery of new oilfields had been dropping for decades. Chance factors play a large role in oil exploration, and so do political and economic conditions; for many years, these made it possible for the ongoing decline in discoveries to be dismissed as a temporary aberration. As the twentieth century approached its end, though, it was becoming clear that something considerably more serious was going on.

The problem could be stated in very simple terms. The peak year for petroleum discovery worldwide came in 1964, and despite dramatic improvements in technology and herculean efforts on the part of oil companies, rates of discovery of new oilfields had been trending down ever since. By the mid-1980s, global discoveries of oil were no longer keeping pace with extraction, and by the last years of the century annual rates of extraction were running three to four times the volume of annual discoveries. Since oil must be discovered before it can be extracted from the ground, a drop in discovery is the proverbial canary in the coal mine, a harbinger of troubles in the near future. A handful of researchers thus went public with their concerns that, if the trend continued, geological factors might cause the annual rate of extraction to peak and begin to decline and thus would be unable to keep up with potential demand (Campbell & Laherrère, 1998).

These warnings found very few listeners at first. After an initial flurry of attention, the mainstream media ignored the subject, and official bureaucracies tasked with tracking the future of energy treated the possibility of a near-term peak in petroleum production as a non-issue; the US Energy Information Administration, for example, until quite recently estimated how much oil would be produced in the future by calculating the likely increase in demand and then simply assuming an equivalent increase in supply (Heinberg, 2003). Despite this climate of dismissal, those first researchers continued their work and were joined by others, forming an ad hoc network linked mostly by the Internet. In the process, the expected peak of global petroleum production found a new and simpler label: peak oil.

In retrospect, three things about the peak oil movement stand out as significant. The first was the remarkable speed with which efforts to predict the arrival of peak global petroleum production narrowed in on a consistent and, as it turned out, accurate date. Half a dozen teams of researchers, working with publicly available data and using a range of different methodologies, found that their estimates converged in the middle years of the twenty-first century's first decade. Kenneth Deffeyes, a petroleum geologist who was among the influential figures in the early peak oil scene, was partly joking when he predicted Thanksgiving 2005 as the date when peak oil would occur (Deffeyes, 2005). Still, it was a joke with an edge, since most of the estimates from peak oil researchers fell within a few years to either side of that estimate. The edge turned out to be even sharper in hindsight because, as it turned out, 2005 was in fact the year when global petroleum production reached its peak.

The second significant point about the peak oil movement was the extent to which it presented a thoughtful and unsensational view of what would happen as petroleum production peaked and began to decline. While the mainstream media consistently dismissed those who spoke out about peak oil as doomsayers, and the peak oil movement attracted a lively fringe that used peak oil as a frame for the standard range of contemporary apocalyptic fantasies (e.g., Savinar, 2004), the projections offered by Deffeyes, Colin Campbell, Jean Laherrère, and other leading figures in the peak oil movement were remarkably short on hyperbole and predictions of doom. All these writers agreed that the coming of peak oil would pose a serious challenge to industrial society, a challenge with major technological, economic, political, and cultural impacts, but they described that challenge in careful and reasoned terms.

The collision between rising demand for energy and contracting supplies of the modern world's most important fuel, they argued, would drive energy costs sharply upwards, repeating the experience of the 1970s energy crisis on a larger scale and putting serious strains on those nations that did not take steps to prepare for the shock (Campbell, 2004; Deffeyes, 2005). A few peak oil researchers raised the possibility that declining production of the energy resources that made industrial civilization possible might sooner or later make the industrial system itself unsustainable and force a return to some equivalent of pre-industrial technologies and cultural forms (Duncan, 1993; Greer, 2008). Still, the colloquial phrase is also the accurate one in this case: troubling though the prospect of peak oil was, it wasn't the end of the world.

This relatively straightforward point was, however, almost completely lost upon critics of the peak oil thesis. This is the third significant point about the peak oil movement: responses to warnings about the imminence of peak oil from all sides—the liberal and conservative political parties, the industrial and financial spheres, the entire spectrum of social change movements from far left to far right, and the vast majority of ordinary citizens as well—were weirdly detached from the issues that the peak oil movement was attempting to raise. Nearly all these responses misstated the most basic dimensions of the peak oil thesis and used remarkable distortions of logic and evidence to support their claims.

A great many would-be critics insisted, for example, that the peak oil thesis claimed that the world was about to run out of oil, with immediate and cataclysmic results, and pointed to the world's remaining reserves of petroleum as proof that this will not happen. They were, of course, quite correct, as the Hubbert curve shows that roughly half the world's extractable oil will be produced and consumed after the peak of production, and peak oil models take this fact into account. Soaring petroleum prices and fuel shortages caused by decreased production in an oil-hungry world, not the impossible nightmare of a world suddenly running out of oil, drives the difficulties predicted by the peak oil thesis, but that point somehow rarely found its way into these critiques.

Another large body of criticism dealt with—or, more precisely, did not deal with—the steep and ongoing declines in the discovery of new oilfields by treating the new and relatively small fields that were discovered each year as conclusive proof that peak oil was not an issue. In 2000, oilfields around the Caspian Sea were the oil discovery *du jour*; ten years later, the Bakken Shale in North Dakota filled that role. In both cases, and several others in-between, a modest new resource was transformed by wildly optimistic estimates into the illusion of a game-changing event and became the centre of grandiose claims of a new era of energy abundance. In the case of the Caspian Sea fields, those claims sank promptly into oblivion once oil companies moved past the first round of exploratory wells and the overblown initial guesses gave way to a more realistic, and much smaller, picture of the scale of the resource. In the case of the Bakken Shale, that process is just getting under way as of this writing; it will be educational to see how promptly recent claims about shale oil from the Bakken fields flooding the market and crashing the price of petroleum are quietly forgotten in their turn.

THE UNSEEN LIMITS

The third major body of peak oil criticism applied the rhetoric of the second to a series of alternative energy resources. In the late 1990s, pundits on the green end of the cultural spectrum proclaimed a "hydrogen economy" that would soon render petroleum obsolete. A few years later, ethanol from America's cornfields was promoted as the wonder fuel that would prevent any future shortage of petroleum from becoming a problem. After that, it was wind power. As of this writing, methane hydrates and so-called cold fusion seem to be the leading candidates for the next wonder resource that will, in theory, make our energy troubles go away. Plenty of other candidates are available to fill the same role once these prove to be inadequate in their turn.

Some of these technologies, it deserves to be said, will very likely have an important role in the energy mix of the future. Others almost certainly will not. For example, despite trillions of dollars in investment over more than half a century, fusion power is no closer to commercial viability than it was in the 1960s, and there are increasingly good reasons to think that the nearest approach our species will ever make to a working fusion reactor is the 93-million-mile gap separating the earth from the sun (Seife, 2008). Decades of hard work and unwelcome experience in the renewable energy field, though, has shown that none of the alternatives to fossil fuels is capable of providing the same cheap, concentrated, abundant supply of energy that industrial civilization currently gets from fossil fuels, and especially from petroleum. In every case, difficulties with concentration, reliability, and cost impose limits that cannot be evaded.

That was why the renewable energy option explored in the 1970s involved so extensive a commitment to conservation and improved energy efficiency; it is why renewable energy has never been able to compete economically with fossil fuels when the latter are readily available, and why nuclear power has never been commercially viable except when it has been supported by gargantuan direct and indirect government subsidies—made possible, ultimately, by the economy of abundance provided by fossil fuels. That recognition, however, is nowhere to be found in the grandiose plans for hydrogen-fuelled cars, orbiting solar power stations, and biofuel plantations on a continental scale that take up so much space in critiques of peak oil that focus on the supposed prospects for powering the industrial world on alternative energy resources.

This third body of criticism, like the first two, thus avoided dealing with the realities of peak oil by redefining those realities out of existence. All three conjured up imaginary worlds in which limits on the world's access to cheap abundant energy do not exist—in which petroleum is no longer constrained by the geological factors that make the Hubbert curve function, or a limitless sequence of massive new oil discoveries can take place on a finite planet, or the universe is obliged to provide us with some other energy source that can readily replace fossil fuels and simultaneously further an assortment of environmental and social goals. None of these things appears to exist in the world we actually inhabit, to be sure, and yet this does nothing to diminish the enthusiasm with which a comfortable majority of people across the industrial world used such arguments to dismiss the possibility of peak oil from consideration.

That dismissal remains fixed in place as of this writing, even though the predictions offered up by peak oil critics have turned out to be repeatedly and embarrassingly wrong. Consider the assurance, repeated straight across the spectrum of peak oil denial, that if the price of petroleum were to rise significantly, economic forces would inevitably bring something to the rescue and force prices back down. For the first body of critics cited above, that "something" is simply increased production of oil from existing fields, responding to increased prices through the ordinary workings of supply and demand. For the second body, it is the accelerated discovery of new oilfields, while the third has insisted that the rising price of oil would make alternative energy resources competitive and bring them into use on a large scale.

Over the last decade, each of these claims has been put to the test. The average price of oil has climbed dramatically, from around $30 a barrel in 2002 to well over $100 a barrel as of this writing. During that same period, there has been no shortage of efforts to pump more oil from existing fields, discover new fields, and bring alternative energy sources online, but the ample energy supplies that would supposedly become available as a result of rising prices are nowhere to be seen, and the price of oil continues to move raggedly upwards. This is what peak oil researchers have predicted all along: the supply of petroleum and other energy resources is constrained by physical and geological limits, rather than by purely economic factors, and constraints of the former kind cannot be overcome by the workings of a market economy.

Those new energy sources that have been brought on line in recent years, while heavily promoted by the mass media as evidence that peak oil is a non-issue, actually offer far more support to the peak oil camp than to its opponents. Tar sands, grain ethanol, and "tight" oil trapped in shale deposits that can be opened by hydrofracturing ("fracking") technology have been familiar to energy researchers for decades. The reason they were not part of the world's liquid fuels supply until recently is that all three will only yield useful fuel given substantial inputs of fossil fuel energy and raw materials. The tar sands and ethanol industries can afford these inputs at the moment because they receive lavish government subsidies, which spread much of the cost of production via taxation onto other sectors of the economy; the "fracking" industry in the United States is, as of this writing, the beneficiary of a speculative bubble on Wall Street, which is directing many billions of dollars of investment money into shale gas and shale oil projects. In all three cases, claims that these resources will flood the liquid fuels market and drive down prices have proven inaccurate, and it is becoming increasingly hard to dismiss the possibility that the temporary booms in these fuel sources are simply so many signs that the bottom of the liquid fuels barrel is being industriously scraped.

Under normal circumstances, a hypothesis that yields accurate predictions about the future is taken more seriously than competing hypotheses that consistently fail to do so. As peak oil has arrived, however, that has not happened. Instead, authority figures in the economic and energy fields have redoubled their criticism of the peak oil model and insisted on the validity of the very models that have failed so dramatically to anticipate the industrial world's current predicament, while both they and public opinion as a whole have blamed the rising tide of economic trouble that followed the arrival of peak oil on everything but the arrival of peak oil. Thus, it may be worth suggesting that these are not normal circumstances, and that something has gone seriously wrong with the whole suite of processes that industrial societies use to anticipate the future and determine constructive policies in the present.

What has gone wrong with those decision-making processes, in turn, may be readily defined by comparison with the historical examples already cited. It was impossible for post-war American society to grapple with depression and anomie among women without confronting the failure of deeply held and culturally important beliefs about women's place in the world, and it was equally impossible for the antebellum South to make sense of the behaviour of slaves without challenging core elements of the worldview that claimed to justify a slave-holding society. In the same way, it is impossible to understand and respond to the arrival of peak oil without raising hard questions about beliefs that are of vital importance in contemporary society. What is put at risk by peak oil and its consequences is, if anything, closer to the core of today's collective psychology than beliefs in the natural subordination of women to family roles, or of people of African descent to those of European descent, were in their day. It is not going too far, in fact, to describe the structure of beliefs, attitudes, and presuppositions challenged by peak oil as the central myth of the modern industrial world.

TWO
The religion of progress

The mere suggestion that modern industrial civilization has myths of its own risks misunderstanding, if not flat rejection. In current popular usage, the English word "myth" and its cognates in other Western languages have come to mean "a story that is not true", and a great deal of contemporary thought uses this redefinition to ground a core distinction between modern and pre-modern societies: the latter supposedly based their worldviews on stories that are not true, while we base ours on true narratives revealed by science. One genre of social criticism has gone so far as to point to a supposed pathological lack of myths in modern societies as a cause of social and psychological problems (May, 1991; Rue, 1989).

More than a century ago, Max Muller showed considerably greater insight when he wrote, "Depend on it, there is mythology now as there was in the time of Homer, only we do not perceive it, because we ourselves live in the very shadow of it, and because we all shrink from the full meridian light of truth" (Muller, 1882, p. 353). The two obscuring factors he cited—the overshadowing influence of a living myth on the thought of those who accept it as valid, and the fear of a confrontation with truth unmediated by the familiar forms of the myth—remain as much live issues in our time as they were in his.

Any understanding of myth must begin with a sense of the role of narrative in human society and the human mind. Narratives may be humanity's oldest tools, and they are certainly among the most powerful; it is by relating the diverse events of life together in narrative structures that we each reduce what William James termed "the blooming, buzzing confusion" (James, 1890, p. 462) of unfiltered experience into an ordered and understandable cosmos. Any statement about meaning, from the simplest to the most profound, is effectively a statement about narrative structure. The narratives central to a society's sense of meaning, in turn, are those that may properly be called myths.

It may be useful here to consider how these basic narratives worked in another historical setting. Most Greeks of the time of Homer, for example, would have rejected the claim that the traditional account of, say, the conflict between Zeus and the Titans was a myth in the modern colloquial sense of the word—that is, a story that is not true. In Homer's works, the word *μυθος*—the root of our word "myth"—normally meant a recitation of remembered events, and this definition presupposes that the events that are remembered and recited—because they are worth remembering and reciting—are true, or at least more likely true than otherwise.

The Titanomachy—the mythic conflict just mentioned—was just such a recitation. Despite the lack of concrete evidence or eyewitness accounts to back the claim that this conflict took place, its reality was supported by the definitions of truth commonly accepted in Homer's time: the story was ancient, it was vouched for by people generally recognized as wise, and so on. It was also a plausible story, the kind of story that people of the time could readily accept as true, because it had close parallels in other, more familiar contexts.

Though nobody in Homer's Greece had personally observed Zeus hurling thunderbolts at Titans, for example, the story of a young and vigorous heir taking the throne of a petty kingdom and cracking the heads of rebellious vassals of an older generation must have been as commonplace at that time as it has normally been in other feudal societies. The thought that the Titanomachy might simply have projected the social habits of their culture and age onto the inkblot patterns of the cosmos would likely have seemed far-fetched to the Homeric Greeks, had anyone thought to suggest it to them. For those living in the shadow of the myth, it must have seemed far more reasonable to take the Titanomachy as a valid account of a defining event in the history of the cosmos, and its reflections in the politics of the time as evidence that, in fact, the cosmos was the kind of place where things like the Titanomachy happened.

Such reconstructions of the faith and worldview of Homer's time are speculative, to be sure, but the speculation gains considerable support from the parallel role of a different narrative with a comparable place in the modern industrial world. This latter narrative, like the Titanomachy, includes events that no living observer has actually witnessed, but it is generally considered true, for most of the same reasons that the Titanomachy was accepted. It gains plausibility from the fact that events similar to those the narrative describes have been witnessed by many people, so that a reasonable case can be made that the cosmos is the kind of place where things like the modern narrative can be expected to happen.

The possibility that this may show the projection of cultural contents onto the cosmos seems just as improbable to many people today as a similar suggestion would have seemed to the Homeric Greeks. The one major difference between the Titanomachy and the modern narrative is that Zeus' battle with the Titans was projected onto the distant past, while the modern narrative projects its most important scenes onto the future.

The narrative in question is the story of progress: the belief that all human history is a linear trajectory that has risen up from the squalor and misery of the prehistoric past through ever-ascending stages of increased knowledge, prosperity, enlightenment, and technological sophistication, and will inevitably continue to do so into a limitless future. The narrative of progress has complex historical roots (Nisbet, 1980), and its path to its present role as the most influential myth of modernity—more specifically (as will be discussed further on), as the central religious myth of our time—was by no means straightforward. Nor, of course, is it without its critics, its heresies, or competing narratives that offer up alternative ways of understanding the cosmos. The same points could be made with equal justice of the dominant myth of any society.

In its most overtly mythic form, at the hands of such popularizers of science as the late Carl Sagan (Sagan, 1980), the narrative of progress becomes very nearly theological in tone, a grand vision of origins and destiny that traces the journey of humanity from the caves to the stars. In these versions of the myth, the vague but emotionally compelling vision of a future of endless betterment takes centre stage as a justification for present conditions and an incentive towards actions that support certain interests over others. Still, even those versions of the narrative that copy the framework of religious myth in a less robust manner serve similar ends; it is not at all hard to trace the social, political, and economic implications of a belief system that presupposes, for example, that newer techniques are better than older ones just because they are newer, and that ideas are not merely rendered unfashionable but actually disproved by the mere passage of time.

Central to the myth of progress, and also one of the keys to its potent emotional appeal, is its affirmation of the omnipotence of human agency. The myth of progress includes the belief that whatever obstacles stand in the way of humanity's advance towards an endless series of brighter futures must inevitably be overcome, if not now, then in some future period. People living in a society that defines itself as advanced and progressing, and who embrace the myth of progress as a true description of the world, thus participate vicariously in omnipotence. However straitened their own circumstances and options may be, they can console themselves with the belief that their descendants, or at least other human beings who come after them, will not be so burdened. Where the Titanomachy justified the social and psychological order of the classical world by a comparison with an imagined past of chaotic forces run wild, the myth of progress accomplishes the same apologetic task by looking in two directions—first, towards an imagined past of primitive squalor and misery that is portrayed as much worse than even the most difficult parts of the present, and, second, towards an imagined future of endless betterment in which all of today's sufferings and injustices will turn out to have been necessary steps on the path towards humanity's glorious destiny.

The pervasive and passionate modern belief in the goodness and inevitability of progress underlies a great many otherwise confusing phenomena in contemporary life, and the blindness to the imminent threat of peak oil discussed in Chapter One is among the most striking of these. To grasp how that blindness works, and to understand how the myth of progress sets the stage for an abundance of personal and collective psychological dysfunctions, it may be useful to begin with a glance at the psychological dimensions of myth in general.

THE PSYCHOLOGY OF MYTH

Psychological interest in the nature and structure of mythology dates from the early days of the depth psychology movement, and the two leading figures of that movement—Sigmund Freud and Carl Jung—both gave interpretations of myth an important role in their explorations of the deep structure of the human psyche. For Freud, myths expressed typical patterns of human relationship in a form stripped of the euphemisms and sublimations that render these same patterns opaque in everyday life. The myth of Oedipus, for instance, embodies central but unmentionable aspects of human family relationships: the erotic dimension of the bond between son and mother, the sexual rivalry that ensues between son and father, and the repression and sublimation of both these factors by the superego of the son. The tangled emotions set in process by these drives repeat themselves covertly in every family, but, according to Freud, they were acted out overtly in prehistoric times, leaving enduring cultural traces that can be found in the world's religions and mythologies (Freud, 1912–13).

From this standpoint, myth thus functions as a socially acceptable way of acknowledging personal and collective conflicts too painful to confront in any more direct manner. In the myth of Oedipus—to return to Freud's most famous example—every man's erotic desire for his mother and sexual jealousy towards his father are portrayed openly, but in an impersonal and therefore emotionally safe manner. Oedipus as Everyman acts out the fantasy of killing his father and marrying his mother, and he is then destroyed by the consequences of his deeds, giving the superego the final word in the drama. The catharsis that Aristotle describes as the essential effect of tragedy (in Bywater, 1952) thus purges the psyche of the accumulated stress built up by the insoluble conflict between the desires of the id and the rules of the superego. Other myths get the same effect in other ways—through laughter in the case of comic myth, for example, and through vicarious triumph in the case of heroic myth.

The same concept of myth as expression of the typically human also underlies Jung's theory of mythology, though the Jungian approach develops that insight in its own way. To Jung, the personalities and situations of myth are not simply reflections of typical human situations, but expressions of autonomous contents of the psyche, which are themselves the subjective reflections of instinctual drives that are found in all human beings and descend ultimately from the pre-human past. These reflections or archetypes exist on a level of mental process—the collective unconscious—that cannot be accessed directly by consciousness, but projects its contents in veiled forms into human thought, art, dreams, and myths (Jung, 1968).

Though terminology and emphases differ, the same crisis in psychological development that Freud interpreted through the myth of Oedipus can be explored in an equally mythic manner using Jung's theories. For Jung as for Freud, the mother is the first object of the son's libido. The refocusing of erotic desire away from the mother, however, is in Jung's view not simply a matter of repression and sublimation on the part of the troubled and terrified child; it also reflects autonomous processes within the depths of the psyche through which the anima—the archetype of woman as lover—differentiates itself from the mother-archetype, so that it may eventually be projected on a woman of the son's own generation. From a Jungian perspective, narratives such as the story of Parsifal, in which the son leaves his mother and seeks a princess, a feminine symbol such as the Holy Grail, or both, reflect that process in the language of myth (Jung & von Franz, 1972).

Important theoretical and therapeutic issues turn on the differences between Freud's and Jung's theories. For the purposes of this study, however, these are less important than the core insight shared by the two approaches: that myths are emotionally powerful narratives that draw their enduring appeal from within the psyche, rather than from any necessary concordance with particular details of the outside world. Another way of saying the same thing is that myths are not necessarily about the things they appear to be about. What gives them their power and durability, and makes them myths rather than passing fancies, is that they refer covertly to something other than their apparent subject, and thus express in symbolic form what either must not (to Freud) or cannot (to Jung) be expressed more directly. The myth of Oedipus thus presents itself as a story about things that happened to a particular man in Greece a long time ago, but what matters about it is that it repeats itself in the childhood of every man—as, in turn, does the choice faced by the young Parsifal as he decides whether to stay at home with his mother or venture out into the world to encounter his destiny.

The myth of the Titanomachy, in the same way, was not

important to the people of ancient Greece because of its apparent meaning, as an account of certain events that were believed to have happened at a particular moment in the prehistoric past. Its importance came from what it said covertly and indirectly about the social context in which it was believed, and to which its believers applied it. Like the myth of Oedipus, the story of Zeus' defeat of the Titans has a personal and developmental dimension—it reflects the triumph of every child-become-adult who successfully establishes his or her own life in the face of the conflicting expectations of the older generation.

In ancient Greece and Rome, however, it took on a further dimension of meaning as a core justification for the way society was organized. Throughout the history of the classical world, from the Archaic period in Greece to the twilight years of the Roman Empire, the image of a single charismatic figure uniting a community, overcoming the turbulent powers of chaos, and establishing an ordered cosmos had immense psychological appeal. It pervaded politics, for example, becoming a standard justification for any number of enlightened and unenlightened despotisms; it all but defined the structure of ancient Greek and Roman family life; and it gave impetus to one of the most characteristic cultural projects of the age—the pursuit of philosophy as a way of life in which reason quelled the discordant passions and imposed order on the little cosmos of the self (Hadot, 1998).

Across the spectrum of human experience, from the most public and collective realm to the most private and personal, the myth of the Titanomachy thus reflected itself in the most fundamental patterns of classical society. Since many aspects of human experience do not work well when approached in the manner that the myth would suggest—it is not always helpful to treat every source of disturbance as a chaotic force that ought to be hammered into obedience, nor is centralization of power a good thing in every case—mapping the Titanomachy onto the cosmos tolerably often becomes a source of trouble, on personal, familial, or social levels. Since the myth contains its own interpretation of such difficulties, however, believers in the myth tended to see these troubles as proof that the powers of chaos had not yet been sufficiently beaten into submission, and they responded to the failure of the mythic model by attempting to impose the model even more forcibly than before.

In times of crisis on any level of society, those responses that followed the lead of the Titanomachy were therefore much more likely to be attempted than those that followed alternative paths, even when attempts to follow the Titanomachy model had proven repeatedly ineffective and other, more promising options were ready to hand. The waning years of the Roman Empire are a case in point. As the Empire faltered, the imperial government responded by centralizing power and imposing increasingly burdensome controls on every aspect of life in the Roman world. Even though these controls caused more problems than they solved, the compulsion to play Jupiter proved to be too strong for most emperors to resist. The replacement of traditional Pagan religion with Christianity did nothing to weaken the narrative: Christ Pantocrator took the place of Jupiter, an assortment of fallen angels replaced the Titans, and the same narrative under a different label continued to drive events to an unwelcome end.

This fixation on a counterproductive narrative had immediate practical consequences. Sociologist Joseph Tainter has pointed out that by the late Empire, the complexity of Roman imperial government had passed so far beyond the point of diminishing returns that each new layer of complexity had negative returns in terms of benefits to the system and eventually overloaded the structure to the point that a series of relatively minor shocks brought it crashing down (Tainter, 1988). Yet emperors and their advisors repeatedly failed to grasp this, since the mythic framework that pervaded their thinking made any response other than increasing the total burden of centralized control unthinkable.

HAVE WE PROGRESSED?

The implied comparison of the contemporary belief in progress to the Titanomachy, or any myth generally recognized as such, invites the misunderstanding and denial invoked at the beginning of this chapter. To most people in the contemporary industrial world, after all, progress is not a myth but a fact. Still, a strong case can be made that belief in the inevitability and goodness of progress not only serves many of the same social and psychological functions in modern industrial culture as myths such as the Titanomachy did in their day, but also represents a picture of reality no more complete—and thus a source of practical guidance no more useful—than Greek and Roman myth.

Any such exploration of progress, of course, has to begin with a recognition of the fact that many people in the modern world have experienced a great deal of what passes for progress in their own lives. In the world's industrial nations, certainly, nearly everyone alive has seen a plethora of newer and more complex technologies replace older and simpler ones. There are still people alive today in the industrial world who recall the first time an automobile drove through their town; there are many more who watched the television the day human beings first set foot on the moon. The days before cell phones and the Internet are well within the memories of most of today's adult population. Further back in history, at least to a certain point, the same process can be seen at work: the development of steam power from the first crude coal-fired pumping engines in the early years of the eighteenth century, for example, and its transformation from a convenience for coal miners to the dominant power source of a civilization, provide forceful support to the narrative of progress.

Trace history back much further than those early steam engines, however, and it becomes much harder to find examples that fit the narrative except by a drastic compression of historical time and a studied inattention to any detail that contradicts the myth. During the seventeenth century, for example, it was considered a question worth debating in France and Britain whether the European nations of that time had advanced any further than ancient Greece or Rome; while the issues on which that debate centred were cultural rather than technological, the same argument could have proceeded equally well on a technological basis (DeJean, 1997). As recently as 1939, as Winston Churchill famously remarked, the fraction of British houses with central heating was smaller than it had been in Roman times (Churchill, 1956).

A strong case can be made, in fact, that relative technological stasis was far more evident than any noticeable progressive trend over the millennia from the emergence of the first urban societies to the coming of the industrial revolution. It is worth noting, for example, the extent to which the lives of ordinary people—priests, soldiers, and farmers—in the France of Louis XIV were comparable to those of equivalent people in the Egypt of Ramses II, three thousand years earlier. In both nations, and in every other relatively complex society across the centuries that separated them, human and animal muscle provided most of the available energy for economic activity, supplemented with small amounts of additional energy from renewables such as wind and water. The hard limits imposed by these energy sources restricted economic surpluses to a tiny fraction of what is standard in today's industrial societies, and the very modest surpluses that existed were monopolized by the ruling elite for vanity projects such as the Palace of Versailles or the Temple of Karnak. Even in the realms of symbolism and collective psychology, parallels are easy to find—to begin with, for example, both nations even had a Sun King.

Between 8000 BCE, when the development of grain agriculture first made it possible to produce the surpluses needed to build and maintain urban societies, and 1700 CE, when the first stirrings of the industrial revolution set in, the common pattern shared by ancient Egypt and early modern France represented the zenith of human social and technological complexity. Efforts to push beyond that level were infrequent, and typically collapsed in short order as the available supply of energy and material wealth proved inadequate to maintain any more complex system. These urban agricultural societies, furthermore, only thrived in regions of the Earth's surface that were particularly favourable to such projects.

Elsewhere, three older systems—tribal village cultures that practised horticulture and sedentary animal raising; nomadic herding cultures that roamed many of the world's great grasslands; and the hunter-gatherer economy, the oldest of all—occupied their own ecological niches. Even in the Old World, where urban agricultural societies appeared earliest, these simpler human ecologies occupied at least half the total inhabited land even in those periods when urban societies were at their most successful. Glance back before the emergence of the first urban agricultural societies to the 99% or so of human history in which the hunter-gatherer economy was the norm, and the last trace of progress vanishes from sight; the stone toolkits used by Cro-Magnon societies in Ice Age France 30,000 years ago, for example, were as complex and efficient as those used by hunter-gatherers at the dawn of the modern era.

Insofar as progress happened at all before 1700, in other words, it took place in brief and relatively localized bursts, most of which ended—as ancient Egypt and the Roman Empire did, for instance—in steep declines to a less complex technological and social level. A few of these bursts of progress did spawn new technological, economic, and social ventures that proved lasting and spread gradually across those parts of the world that had the ecological conditions necessary to support them. Most other ventures did not, and the frequency with which archaeologists have uncovered ruined cities swallowed by the jungle or buried in the desert sands offers a useful reminder of the fragility of even the more successful products of human social evolution. As a general rule, furthermore, decline has been as common in history as progress, and long periods of relative stasis far more common than either.

The accelerating linear trend of technological progress that has characterized the period since 1700, in other words, is an unusual event in human history. It is not quite unprecedented: other ages of expansion and abundance have taken place whenever human societies were able to access a large body of previously untapped resources. These precedents have a stark warning to offer, however, since the great majority of them ended in precipitous decline when the newly tapped resource base was used at a rate faster than natural processes could replenish it and was exhausted. History is littered with the wreckage of once-successful societies that followed this path into time's dustbin: up with the rocket, down with the stick (Ponting, 1992).

From the perspective of history, in fact, our current industrial civilization is simply a re-enactment of this familiar pattern on a larger scale. The resource base that the first industrial nations accessed in the years following 1700—the fossil fuels stored up inside the earth over the half a billion years before that time—was far richer than any previous example, and thus it drove a far more drastic expansion of prosperity and political power than any earlier civilization had been able to achieve. The coming of peak oil, however, marks the point at which our modern example reaches its zenith and begins the long descent to a much lower level of technological and social complexity, following the course of those previous examples.

The most reasonable hypothesis concerning the future of industrial society would thus seem to be that the three centuries of expansion set in motion by the industrial revolution will be followed in turn by an extended period of economic contraction and technological retrenchment, driven by the exhaustion of the fossil fuel supplies that powered the expansion. Whether or not the availability of abundant fossil fuels was a sufficient cause for the boomtime of industrialism, this hypothesis suggests, some equally abundant supply of highly concentrated, easily accessed energy is a necessary condition; in its absence, the lavish lifestyles and complex technologies of the industrial age will no longer be viable. As fossil fuel reserves deplete and the industrial world is forced to make do with the diffuse, intermittent, and expensive energy sources that are left, our relative prosperity will give way to something closer to the more stringent economic realities of other times, and only those technologies that can be maintained on a much less extensive resource base of energy and materials than the one we have at present can be expected to survive into the de-industrial future (Greer, 2008).

Reasonable as it is, however, that hypothesis is nowhere to be found on the conceptual maps of contemporary society. Instead, the only alternative to continued progress that most people in the industrial world are able to imagine is some form of apocalyptic catastrophe vast enough to stop progress in its tracks, and even then it is commonly supposed that progress will resume again once the rubble stops bouncing. The possibility of gradual decline, common though it is as a historical phenomenon, is sufficiently unthinkable that it plays no role in meaningful planning for the future. As a result, the practical steps that would make the downside of Hubbert's peak less difficult, and ensure the preservation of many of the benefits of the recent past, are not even being considered, much less put into effect.

Instead, industrial societies around the world behave as though a future of continued technological advance, economic expansion, and global socio-political integration is guaranteed, and projects that will only make sense if such a future were to happen—for example, massive expansions of airport facilities and major road systems—proceed apace, even in regions where by most measures decline has already begun. The possibility that progress may be a temporary and self-limiting phenomenon specific to brief periods in human history remains unthinkable for most people in the modern world. This is the result of the role of progress as a contemporary mythology—and as the basis for a widely accepted modern religion.

THE CIVIL RELIGION OF PROGRESS

By and large, men do not kill their fathers, marry their mothers, and point to the myth of Oedipus to justify their actions. In the waning years of the Roman Empire, by contrast, emperors did indeed try to re-enact the myth of the Titanomachy, and references to Jupiter's triumph over the Titans featured tolerably often in the panegyrics composed by their court poets to celebrate their increasingly infrequent successes over the barbarian invasions that were a prime symptom of Rome's impending collapse. In recent decades, believers in the modern myth of progress have done much the same thing as did Roman emperors, invoking such modern mythic narratives as the Manhattan Project and the Apollo moon landings to justify their efforts to progress out of crises that progress itself has created.

Those narratives that play a central role in any given culture as guides and justifications for action can be called, without too much misunderstanding, the religious myths of that culture, and they form the basis for the culture's religions. In order to understand this use of that much-vexed term "religion", it is necessary to remember that what defines the religions of a culture, and the religious myths that frame them, is not the presence of gods, souls, or other supernatural entities in the institutions and narratives in question. What defines a myth as religious is precisely that it links back (in Latin, *religare*) the individuals who make up the community, and the community itself, to values that the community considers so self-evident and important that they stand outside the sphere of reasonable debate—in a word, values that are sacred.

The concept of civil religion, in the sense the phrase is usually given nowadays, was introduced by sociologist Robert Bellah in a widely cited paper (Bellah, 1967). Borrowing the term from Rousseau but giving it a substantially new meaning, Bellah defined civil religion as a body of beliefs, practices, and symbols expressing values that have no reference to supernatural beings but are considered sacred by a community—in the specific case cited in his article, the national community of the United States. In American public life, he pointed out, documents such as the Declaration of Independence, individuals such as George Washington, symbols such as the national flag, and beliefs such as the superiority of American democracy over other political systems play a role that can only be compared to the role of sacred documents, persons, symbols and beliefs in the life of the believer in an organized religion.

In the years after Bellah's paper first went to press, the concept of civil religion became a widely used interpretive tool in American sociology, and a sense of the diverse forms of civil religion—one might even say, borrowing a phrase from William James, of the varieties of civil religious experience—has become widespread in the field. In the works of a range of recent scholars, most particularly historian of technology David Nye, the recognition of technological progress as a civil religion has become an important theme. The atmosphere of frankly religious awe that has so often surrounded the major spectacles of technology, as Nye has pointed out, fills many of the same collective functions in the modern world as established religions have done in other societies and times (Nye, 1996).

The power of the myth of progress as a religious myth, as already suggested, stems in large part from the sense of vicarious omnipotence it confers on its believers, and the hope of a vicarious salvation it holds out, if not to them, then to their descendants or to humanity in the far future. To a believer in progress, the sense of power and the hope of a future of endless betterment is reinforced by both grand spectacles of technological accomplishment such as spacecraft flights and everyday encounters with technological achievements not available to earlier generations. Today's faithful may not themselves have the opportunity to ride a rocket into space or live in a future in which illness and want are things of the past, but the existence of the former and the promise of the latter serve, as civil religions normally serve, to justify otherwise troubling features of contemporary life. Every religion—civil or otherwise—depends for its psychological power on its ability to help its faithful believers to feel themselves part of something that is greater than themselves, whether that be the totemic spirit of a family or the universal Body of Christ. To the believer in progress, that greater whole is humanity itself, as it traces out its grand trajectory from the caves to the stars.

The psychological power of the civil religion of progress can be traced in the very words we use to discuss technological change. To describe anything as "progressive" is to define it as good in every relevant sense; only in the harshest of ironic terms is it possible, say, to describe a social or technological trend as progressing towards disaster. Words such as "static" and "regressive" have correspondingly negative meanings in contemporary parlance. Consider the way that nations are classed as developed, developing, and underdeveloped, depending on the extent to which their economies have adopted industrial models; the suggestion that certain nations might be overdeveloped, valid though it arguably may be, is unlikely to be taken up in public discourse any time in the near future.

For a further example, consider the way that hunter-gatherer peoples in today's world are described as "still in the Stone Age", while societies not yet industrialized are often stigmatized as "stuck in the Middle Ages", waiting for industrial development to "bring them into the twenty-first century". From a less mythologized standpoint, hunter-gatherer bands and non-industrial agricultural communities are as much a part of the twenty-first century as the most Internet-saturated upscale neighbourhoods of the industrial world. Few turns of phrase reveal more clearly the conviction, all but universally accepted in industrial societies today, that all of human history is a prologue that leads directly and inevitably to us—that is, to the specific social, political, and economic forms of contemporary industrial society—and through us to a future that looks like today's industrial societies but even more so.

One effective way to see the essentially religious and mythological nature of those convictions is to envision a future in which the convictions in question turn out to be wrong. Imagine, for example, that the three centuries of rapid technological development that have created today's industrial societies do in fact prove to be one of the many dead ends of human history. As fossil fuels run short and alternative energy sources fail to provide adequate replacements for them, the world's developed nations plunge into intractable economic depression and political chaos. Meanwhile, many of the nations now considered underdeveloped are able, after a brief if difficult period of sharp population contraction and urban collapse, to stabilize at something close to their present, and much more modest, levels of economic and technical development.

Let us say that, by the last months of 2099, it has become clear that the non-industrial nations of south Asia, Africa, and Latin America, not the formerly prosperous and now bankrupt and fragmented industrial nations, are riding the wave of the future. Village farming communities, economies geared towards local production, and small-scale renewable technologies, providing standards of living comparable to those of today's Third World nations, are becoming the global norm, as a century of futile attempts to find an energy source to replace oil and get technological progress moving again has finally made it clear that the age of superhighways and moon landings is never coming back. As the new century dawns, pundits in Djakarta and Bogotá give interviews to the media explaining that the overdeveloped nations are still stuck in the industrial age and are waiting for de-industrialization to bring them into the twenty-second century!

Propose to most people in the modern industrial world that this scenario represents a possible future, of course, and you can expect fierce disagreement, if not blank incomprehension. It matters not at all that the vision of the future just outlined requires far fewer improbabilities than its more popular rivals; the scenario just sketched, for example, does not require the extraction of infinite fossil fuel supplies from a finite planet, nor does it require some new and presently unknown energy source at least as concentrated, abundant, and convenient as petroleum to make an appearance on cue. A future of the sort sketched out in the thought experiment given above may be possible, even probable, but, within the modern industrial worldview, it is not thinkable.

The widespread contemporary faith in the civil religion of progress is the factor that makes such futures impossible for most people to imagine. That religion has no place for a future in which today's Third World shows the direction in which history is headed, or for any future whatsoever in which today's industrial nations can no longer claim to be the vanguard of humanity, entitled to their current economic and political advantages over other nations because they have progressed further along the path that all humanity supposedly must follow. That history might be headed somewhere else, or, worse yet, might have no direction at all, is a challenge to the most basic—and thus, to the believer in the religion of progress, the most sacred—presuppositions of the belief in progress; it denies both the future of endless betterment that is the secular heaven of that belief system and the future of apocalyptic mass death that is its secular hell.

Peak oil, if its consequences are taken as seriously as they deserve, poses exactly such a challenge to the religion of progress. If, as seems increasingly likely, petroleum turns out to be the most abundant, convenient, and concentrated energy source our species will ever know, and all future human societies will have to make do with less lavish energy sources, then progress as we have known it will end in our lifetimes. Not since Nietzsche announced the death of God has a proclamation so unpalatable disturbed the modern world, yet no messenger so colourful and obtrusive as Nietzsche's madman shouting in the marketplace brings peak oil's message of the death of progress.

Instead, rising energy costs, economic contraction, and social dysfunction carry the unwelcome news into the marketplace of modernity, and it has so far proven tolerably easy for most people in the industrial world either to ignore their message or to reinterpret it in terms more congenial to the myth of progress and other contemporary habits of thought. How long that will continue to be possible, and what the costs will be of persevering in that denial, are other questions entirely.

THREE
The psychology of the progress myth

Those religions that place their hopes in realms and beings that transcend ordinary human experience have certain advantages that are not shared by the civil religions discussed in the previous chapter. Even if the central hope of Christianity turns out to be wholly misplaced, for example, no Christian has to worry about having to face so daunting a prospect anywhere this side of the grave. The fulfilment of the Christian message, with its promise of redemption from sin and death through the sacrifice and resurrection of Jesus Christ, is by most branches of the tradition firmly relegated to the afterlife, where it cannot easily be tested by those who are still among the living.

That same habit of taking refuge in the unverifiable applies equally well to the apocalyptic side of the same faith. While the Second Coming is supposed to happen in the world of everyday experience, Christian churches have shown impressive ingenuity in redefining those scriptural prophecies that appear to date it to no more than a generation or so after the lifetime of Jesus. In this way, the fulfilment of prophecy has been moved off into the indefinite future, where the eye of faith can behold it but that of critical scrutiny cannot.

Civil religions have a much more difficult time accomplishing the same feat. The fate of Communism, one of the twentieth century's most successful evangelical civil religions, offers a cautionary example along these lines. During the wilderness years of that faith—from the 1848 publication of *The Communist Manifesto* by Karl Marx and Friedrich Engels to Lenin's seizure of power in Russia in 1917—its missionaries could describe the glorious future that would arrive "come the revolution" in the most Utopian terms imaginable, without risk of contradiction by events. In the years following the October Revolution, though, as Communist regimes spread to encompass nearly half the population of the globe, the expectation that these glowing promises would at some point be fulfilled became an increasingly problematic issue for the faithful.

The excesses of Lenin and Stalin in Russia, and their equivalents in other Communist nations, could at first be excused by believers as harsh but temporary necessities in the struggle against reactionary elements, but that expedient had a limited shelf life. As one workers' paradise after another turned into a bleak bureaucratic police state that showed no sign of following the Communist prophecy and withering away, it became harder for even the most devout to find ways to justify the gap between theory and practice, and that gap ultimately became a chasm wide enough to swallow the Soviet Union and most of its satellite nations whole. Where religions with a transcendent focus routinely span the millennia—Christianity's run of nearly 2,000 years so far is by no means exceptional—the Communist civil religion thus managed to endure as a significant presence for only a little over 150 years.

A fate of a similar kind may well lie in wait for the civil religion of progress. While historians of the idea of progress have traced its origins back ultimately to classical times, its place in Western societies as a civil religion dates only from the seventeenth century (Nisbet, 1980). Most of the thinkers who popularized the concept of progress in its earliest years interpreted it as an expression of divine providence and thus assimilated it into older religious forms. By the middle of the eighteenth century, however, in the minds of a growing number of people around the world, it had stopped being a gift of God and turned into a replacement for Him. Hopes of the kind usually assigned to the theological sphere gathered around the idea of human progress; its missionaries proclaimed that poverty, disease, and war would inevitably fall before the triumphant march of humanity towards an ever more splendid future; human beings would fly through the air, travel to the Moon, master the forces of nature, and brush aside the limits of space and time; gleaming cities would rise in which every inhabitant could expect the instant fulfilment of every human need and want. Those of my readers whose memories reach back to the 1960s will remember that such promises still played a significant role in the popular literature and media of the time.

It would be easy enough, looking back at those predictions from the perspective of a more cynical age, to dismiss these claims as empty propaganda. Perhaps the most impressive feature of the civil religion of progress, though, was the extent to which, at least for a time, it succeeded in making its prophecies come to pass. For most of three centuries, those who put their faith in progress saw that faith justified by results significantly more often than not. Some of the predicted victories proved to be elusive, to be sure, but a great many of the promises were fulfilled: starvation and extreme destitution became relatively uncommon in the industrial world; many once-common illnesses were conquered by medical science; standards of living in most of the world's industrial nations by and large rose so far that people whose great-grandparents lived in squalid urban tenements or rural hovels without hope of improvement could, by and large, expect to live in decent housing, receive a basic education and at least some medical care, and even purchase a few luxuries. That all this may sound like faint praise shows the extraordinary gulf that separates modern industrial societies from their antecedents three short centuries ago; in the world of 1700, the thought that people at the lower end of the working classes could aspire to any of the things just named would have appeared hopelessly utopian.

It was precisely changes of this kind that gave the civil religion of progress its place as an unquestioned psychological reality in most industrial nations. Until quite recently, believers in the myth of progress could bolster their faith with so many triumphant successes within living memory that the failures were easy to dismiss as irrelevancies. Those visionaries who peered into the future from the vantage point of 1700, imagining a world revolutionized by the advance of technology and science, turned out to be far better prophets than the sceptics who dismissed their hopes as so many ravings.

Still, as investment houses nowadays like to put in the fine print, past performance is no guarantee of future earnings. The industrial revolution was able to provide three centuries of relative abundance to the inhabitants of a favoured minority of the world's nations because it took place on a planet that was still richly stocked with natural resources, especially fossil fuels that embodied millions of years of concentrated solar energy in easily accessible and highly useful forms. It was this untapped abundance that made it possible for the mythic vision of progress towards limitless material betterment to come true, at least for a time, just as it is the exhaustion of that abundance that is bringing that dream to an end. As the course of history begins to drift away from the myth, those who have placed their hopes for the future on the civil religion that grew up around the dream of perpetual progress face a shattering disillusionment, of a kind that has seen extensive discussion in the literature of social psychology.

THE PSYCHOLOGY OF PREVIOUS INVESTMENT

In the autumn of 1954, a suburban Chicago housewife turned trance channeller named Dorothy Martin announced to the world that North America was about to be destroyed. On 21 December of that year, according to the extra-terrestrial intelligences with whom she believed she was in contact, vast floods would sweep south from the Arctic and annihilate all life on the continent. The only survivors would be those who were lifted to safety aboard flying saucers; Martin and her circle of followers expected to be among these few.

The announcement came to the attention of a team of sociologists from the University of Minnesota, who sent graduate students to join the group under false pretences and keep a detailed record of what happened. The result was one of the classics of American sociological literature, *When Prophecy Fails* (Festinger, Riecken, & Schachter, 1956), among the best accounts in print of what happens when a group of believers has to face the complete failure of its belief system. The researchers looked on while Martin—renamed "Marion Keech" in the book—and her followers took her prediction with utmost seriousness and followed to the letter the instructions they believed they had been given by alien intelligences. The only difficulty they faced was that neither the aliens nor the floodwaters appeared as scheduled.

It is the aftermath of the failed prophecy that makes the story relevant for our present purposes. Logically, confronted with a disproof of this magnitude, the appropriate response would be to admit that a mistake had been made and judge future predictions from the same source in the light of that failure. Human beings, however, are not necessarily logical, and neither was the response of the Martin circle.

Instead of accepting the disconfirmation, they sought and found ways of rationalizing away the failure of the floodwaters and the flying saucers to arrive, and they made enthusiastic efforts to recruit new followers for the group's teachings. When this proved unsuccessful, largely as a result of widespread mockery in the local media, most members drifted away from the group, while Martin left the Chicago area to seek more congenial settings.

Martin herself eventually took the religious name of Sister Thedra, settled in the New Age centre of Sedona, Arizona, and spent the rest of her life channelling further messages from her extra-terrestrial contacts about imminent catastrophes and mass flying-saucer landings. The attempts of more recent prophets such as Harold Camping to convince themselves and others of the validity of their prophetic powers, when these had already been disconfirmed, are further examples of the same phenomenon at work. As the dust dies down from the recent flurry of apocalyptic prophecies surrounding 2012, in turn, a bumper crop of similar exercises can be expected.

Baffling though it may seem at first sight, this denial of the obvious is in fact a very common response to the failure of a belief system to make accurate predictions about the world of observable fact. The response becomes intuitively comprehensible once it is remembered that publicly admitting to an error of judgment is a painful act for most people, and the more costly the error in financial, social, or psychological terms, the more painful the admission will be. If admitting a mistake requires severe personal humiliation, the abandonment of values that are central to the personality, or the recognition that the mistake has harmed something or someone that the person who made the mistake loves and values, then the temptation can be strong to deny that the mistake was a mistake—to insist, for example, that the messages channelled by Dorothy Martin were valid communications from extraterrestrial intelligences that should be accepted as true despite the failure of events to conform to them, and to continue to hold this view even in the face of ridicule by unbelievers.

The general term for the pattern of internal conflict that drives such non-rational but profoundly human behaviour patterns is cognitive dissonance (Festinger, 1957). Cognitive dissonance is the experience of conflict between conscious mental contents of any kind—for example, between two beliefs, between a belief and an experience, or between a belief and a habitual behaviour. Such a conflict is a potent source of discomfort; the more severe the conflict, and the more important the mental contents affected by it, the more extreme the discomfort becomes, and those who experience cognitive dissonance are powerfully motivated by that discomfort to reduce it.

The obvious way to reduce the cognitive dissonance between a false prophecy and the experience that proves it false, it might seem, is to reject the prophecy. The difficulty in the case of Martin's followers was that belief in the accuracy of the prophecy was integrated with many other beliefs, habitual behaviours, and other mental contents; to replace belief by disbelief would cause cognitive dissonance between that disbelief and everything else that had previously supported, and been supported by, belief in the prophecy. The simplest way to reduce the total cognitive dissonance was therefore to find some rationalization that would allow the prophecy to remain valid even though the flood did not arrive.

This same quirk of cognitive dissonance can be observed equally in the phenomenon that students of political psychology have termed the backfire effect (Nyhan & Reifler, 2010), in which people respond to evidence disproving a deeply held political belief by affirming the belief all the more forcefully. The same pattern, when it occurs in the economic sphere, is called the sunk cost fallacy (Knox & Inkster, 1968) or the Concorde fallacy (Weatherhead, 1979). The latter term comes from the supersonic jet that went into production despite the studies by the British and French governments showing that the plane had no commercial market and would inevitably be an expensive flop. The fact that so much money had already been invested in the project by the time those studies came in dissuaded both governments from cancelling the plane, even though continuing with the project meant that millions more pounds and francs would be lost in addition to those already wasted.

The history of fusion power, to return to an example already cited, offers another useful example of the Concorde fallacy at work. When work on commercial fusion power began in the 1950s, it was a commonplace claim among physicists and the media alike that fusion reactors would be ready for widespread commercial use within twenty years. As research proceeded, however, serious problems that no one had anticipated began to crop up, the cost of further research skyrocketed, and projections of the cost of fusion power—even assuming that the technology could be made to work at all—quickly showed that it would never be economically viable. Nonetheless, a large and vocal community of fusion researchers whose careers depended on further funding clamoured for more government grants, and politicians kept on finding reasons to provide the funds. Today, after decades of expensive research projects, commercial fusion power is arguably no closer to reality than it was in the 1950s, and yet billions of dollars, pounds, and euros continue to be budgeted each year for the pursuit of a technology that, at this point, seems all but certain never to become viable.

Social critic and peak oil analyst James Howard Kunstler has provided a useful term for the broader cultural equivalent of these personal processes by coining the phrase "the psychology of previous investment" (Kunstler, 2005). Societies, like individuals, make material investments in a variety of projects and tend to make comparable emotional investments in those same projects. Even when a project of this kind has failed according to every objective criterion, a society will quite commonly continue to pursue it, even when this requires the diversion of scarce resources from objectively more important tasks.

The core example cited by Kunstler is the immense investment, material as well as emotional, made by twentieth-century American society in the construction of suburbia. That investment had origins that are not often remembered.

Some amount of suburbanization took place in the 1920s, following the expansion of urban rail and streetcar lines into the countryside, but the great wave of American suburban construction in the 1950s was, as historian Kathleen Tobin showed, largely a strategic response by the US government to the perceived threat of Soviet nuclear bombardment (Tobin, 2002). The dispersal of America's population from compact urban centres into a widely spread suburban pattern was urged on the US government by its strategists and was accomplished through extensive and well-documented policy decisions made by a range of governmental agencies, but it was marketed to consumers on other grounds.

Subsequently, those other grounds—the supposed amenities of suburban living, as described in lavish but not particularly accurate terms by 1950s marketing firms and their successors—entered into American popular culture as largely unquestioned assumptions about the nature of the good life (Kunstler, 1993). Decades after the military justification for suburbia evaporated, and the obvious disadvantages of a system that required most adults to spend long commutes driving from dispersed residences to distant, centralized workplaces and shopping areas had become painfully apparent, even the suggestion that land-use codes be changed to encourage the re-inhabitation of urban centres and small towns and to discourage suburban sprawl remains unthinkable to most Americans. It is indicative that most of the housing built in the United States during the real estate bubble of 2005–2008 took the form of new suburban developments.

The psychology of previous investment is thus a powerful force. It is not, however, omnipotent, and its principal vulnerability has already been mentioned: if it repeatedly makes statements about observable reality that contradict the experience of the believer, the cognitive dissonance between belief and experience builds to the point that abandoning the belief system, despite all the emotional and psychological investment in it, may finally become the least painful option. This is rarely a quick process or a painless one, for those who abandon their past beliefs must not only give up the emotional benefits conferred by those beliefs, but also accept a painfully reordered self-image in which having been wrong suddenly becomes a central feature. In this light, Dorothy Martin's lifelong commitment to a failed belief system becomes understandable: having sacrificed so much for the sake of her beliefs—her home, her place in society, the respect of her friends and neighbours—the thought that she might have done all this in the service of a delusion cannot have been easy even to consider.

The processes explored in this chapter are thus entirely capable of leading otherwise rational people into remarkably irrational behaviour, at least for a time. There are good reasons to believe, however, that the same broad pattern of conflict between reality and its interpretation can have effects that reach beyond the realm of narrowly defined behaviour patterns and lay the foundations for the collapse of the mind into psychosis.

THE DOUBLE BIND

Before the modern vogue for cross-disciplinary studies, it was at least a little unusual for an anthropologist with a background in communications theory to be confronted with the task of making sense of the origins and structure of mental illness. This was the situation, however, in which Gregory Bateson found himself in 1949, when he began work as the staff ethnologist at the Veterans Administration Hospital in Palo Alto, California. His encounters with schizophrenic patients led to a fascination with the extraordinary use of language common in schizophrenia—a "word salad", to use Bateson's phrase, in which the links between word and meaning are stretched past the breaking point by the gravitational force of obsessive patterns of thought that are always present but never openly addressed (Bateson, 1955a).

As one of the pioneers of cybernetics, the science of information transfer, Bateson readily identified the "word salad" as a sign of a distinctive kind of communications failure. Human language, as is well known, takes much of its meaning from a galaxy of nonverbal cues and culturally defined frameworks that give each utterance its proper context and allow it to be interpreted correctly. This is why, to cite a deliberately absurd example, when a male actor in a television soap opera faces the camera and says "I love you", a housewife who watches the programme and hears these words apparently addressed to her can normally be counted on to understand that they are not to be taken as a statement of the actor's feelings towards her. The social constructs that frame the television programme allow her to classify the message correctly as a statement assigned to a fictional character, performed by an actor who very likely does not feel the emotion the words express. Because she has learned to read the contextual cues the soap opera presents to her, she can enjoy the vicarious rush of emotion without taking it personally.

This is exactly the sort of contextualization that schizophrenics consistently get wrong. To borrow one of Bateson's examples, when a schizophrenic patient visits the hospital dining room and is asked by the woman behind the counter, "What can I do for you", he cannot give those words their proper context. Does the clerk intend to do him in, or does she want to have sex with him, or is she simply offering a cup of coffee (Bateson, 1955b)? The schizophrenic cannot tell. His learned inability to read contextual cues causes his attempts at communication and interaction to fail far more often than they succeed. The limited options available to him then include catatonic withdrawal, paranoid reinterpretation of every message according to a rigid interpretive scheme, or any of the other standard forms of full-blown schizophrenia.

It was in the process of exploring the origins of this communications failure that Bateson formulated his theory of the double bind (Bateson, Jackson, Haley, & Weakland, 1956). A double bind is a self-cancelling communication in which verbal meaning is negated by nonverbal cues. Consider, as an example of the sort that Bateson found typical, a parent who verbally demands that a child express affection, but withdraws physically whenever the child tries to do so. The verbal message ("Come give Mommy a kiss") collides with the nonverbal message ("Don't give Mommy a kiss"), and the result is a very confused and anxious child.

If the parent then criticizes the child for not being affectionate, while continuing to repulse any attempt of the child to show affection, the trap closes tight; the child becomes unable to trust his or her own sense of the frame in which the verbal communication takes place. Any attempt by the child to address the double bind directly ("Mommy, if you want a kiss, why did you turn away?") is thrown back on the child in one way or another, so that the real issue—the parent's own unresolved ambivalence towards the child—can never be brought up for discussion. Repeat these patterns over the course of a childhood, Bateson argued, and the likelihood is high that the child will end up both unable to give statements their proper context and subject to explosive emotional strains that make that failure of communication a source of spectacular psychological problems—that is, that he or she will become schizophrenic.

The same problem can be caused in many other ways, of course, but all fit into a specific structure of communication. Bateson's theory argued that a double bind capable of producing schizophrenia can be expressed formally as a set of three injunctions. The first is an overt, verbal demand that some specific behaviour be forthcoming. The second is a covert, nonverbal demand that the first demand should not be obeyed. The third is a covert demand, which may be partly verbal or wholly nonverbal, that the conflict between the first two demands must never be discussed. All three of these demands, in turn, must be backed up by convincing threats, whether those involve violence, parental withdrawal, or some other consequence that the child cannot easily ignore.

The "word salad" of schizophrenic communication is in its own way a creative response to this appallingly difficult situation. The double bind, as Bateson came to see, can be summed up as the experience of being punished for showing any awareness of the real contextual framing of a communication (Bateson, 1960). Schizophrenic language therefore provides the listener with no information about how it is to be interpreted, and the spectrum of schizophrenic behaviours serve the same function in the nonverbal realm by refusing to participate in the ordinary framework of meanings that give speech its context.

The Batesonian model of schizophrenia can thus be seen

as an extreme response to a state of cognitive dissonance that cannot be resolved by the person who suffers from it. A child raised in conditions of the kind that foster schizophrenia constantly encounters dissonance but is forbidden either to resolve it by dismissing one or another of the conflicting message, or to confront it openly by asking for clarification. Withdrawal into schizophrenic language and behaviour represents the only available choice that allows the dissonance to be reduced to tolerable levels, or at least avoided.

Such choices are adaptive for the schizophrenic person, since by adopting them he or she is able to minimize direct encounters with the cognitive dissonance that defines his or her life, and avoid being punished for openly recognizing and describing the double bind for what it is. They are not only adaptive but necessary for a child who is growing up in a situation of the kind sketched out above and whose need to maintain a relationship with even the most dysfunctional parent outweighs all other requirements, including those of sanity. Yet the price exacted by that relationship, and the adjustments needed to maintain it, may well result in a complete inability to cope with any other aspect of life.

THE PRICE OF COMMITMENT

There are obvious differences between schizophrenia and the results of the psychology of previous investment, to be sure, but a close look at the relationship between these phenomena strongly suggests that the differences are a matter of degree rather than of kind. The double bind that traps the child of a parent who cannot face her own ambivalence towards parenthood, for example, affects a relationship so central to the child's physical and emotional survival that the response to that double bind spreads out to influence the whole of life in disastrous ways. The double bind that confronted Dorothy Martin and her followers was considerably less global in nature, and it also had its impact on a group of adults who had already learned the skills of putting language into context. This is why Martin's followers went out into the world to proclaim an extra-terrestrial gospel that had already disproved itself rather than, say, spending the rest of their lives rocking back and forth silently in padded rooms.

Despite the difference in scale and effect, however, the structure of the double bind that seized Martin and her followers follows Bateson's outline to a remarkable degree. The first injunction, in Martin's case, was the insistence that the messages Martin believed she was receiving from extra-terrestrial intelligences were to be accepted as what she claimed them to be. The second injunction was the necessity of dealing with the fact that the events predicted by the communications failed to happen. The first of these injunctions, as Bateson's model requires, was a verbal statement and was overtly repeated and reinforced within Martin's group. The second injunction was nonverbal—the non-appearance of the floodwaters and the flying saucers was experienced by the members of the group rather than described to them; within the group, it was also covert—it was not discussed in any straightforward fashion—and it contradicted the meaning of the first injunction.

An equivalent of the third injunction, finally, was provided by the emotional commitment the members of the group had to their belief system. The members of Martin's group were no more able to cope with a straightforward discussion of the contradiction between their belief in the origin and value of Martin's channelled predictions, and the total failure of those predictions to come about, than the dysfunctional parent described above would have been able to tolerate a frank discussion about her own ambivalence towards expressions of affection from her child. Instead, the contradiction was covered over by a less extreme version of the same mechanism that gives rise to schizophrenic "word salad": the original context of the predictions was denied or reinterpreted in a variety of ways, so that the predictions could be re-contextualized in a way that evaded disproof.

The same Batesonian structure can be traced in the other examples of the psychology of previous investment cited above. The mass production and mass marketing of suburbs in the sixty years following the Second World War, for example, involved a classic double bind, and, like many of the double binds Bateson studied in the families of his schizophrenic patients, it unfolded from an unadmitted agenda on the part of those who imposed the double bind—in this case, the issues of nuclear defence explored in the study by Kathleen Tobin cited above.

Because the political and military authorities found it inadvisable to discuss the fact that the relocation of civilian populations out of densely settled urban centres was a matter of strategic expediency, the suburban project was sold to the American people by means of sophisticated advertising campaigns that attributed a higher quality of life to suburban living. This served as the first, verbal and overt, injunction of Bateson's model. The second, covert and nonverbal, injunction was provided by the simple fact that far more often than not, suburban living failed to live up to the expectations heaped upon it by the advertising. Instead, it burdened breadwinners with long commutes and other family members with a socially and emotionally impoverished environment, cut off from the extended family and community ties that most Americans had known in the pre-suburban era—an impoverishment that played out in alcoholism, drug abuse, juvenile delinquency, mental illness, and most of the other standard markers of psychological stress.

The equivalent of the third injunction, finally, was provided by the commitments that made millions of Americans unwilling to admit that the negative consequences just mentioned were products of the suburban lifestyle, since this would require accepting that their financial and emotional investments in suburban homes had been a bad choice, and that the authorities and popular-media figures who had marketed the suburbs to Americans had been lying about its benefits. Like so many other investors confronted with the failure of a prized asset to perform as expected, many inmates of suburbia thus found ways to insist that their investments had been as wise as the advertisements claimed, and that the losses incurred had been the result of factors unrelated to the suburban environment.

Thus the depression and anomie that Betty Friedan described as "the problem that has no name"—which arguably had much to do with the extreme isolation imposed on housewives by suburban living patterns—were blamed instead on gender inequalities that, though quite real, somehow never managed to cause the same epidemic problems in settings that allowed women ample opportunities to maintain rich social interactions outside the family circle on an everyday basis. In the same way, the explosion of adolescent rebellion in the years immediately following America's suburban revolution was blamed on drugs, rock music, and a host of other allegedly bad influences. The possibility that the psychological impact of suburban isolation might have played a major role in driving an entire generation to revolt received very little attention from those for whom, by definition, suburbia equalled the good life.

The consequences of this sort of collective double bind can go considerably beyond either the relatively harmless enthusiasms of Dorothy Martin's followers, on the one hand, or the quiet desperation that drove so many suburban housewives in the 1950s and 1960s to rely on psychiatric medications to get through the day. It is not exactly comforting that the most infamous example of collective madness in recent historical memory, the brutal trajectory of Nazi Germany, can so readily be analysed in the same Batesonian terms.

In Germany after the First World War, the first injunction was provided by the ideology of "*Deutschland über alles*": the insistence—pervasive in German culture for most of a century beforehand—that Germany was destined by Providence to rise to a position of global dominion. The second injunction was the pervasive but unmentionable awareness, driven home by defeat, that in an age of continental superpowers and petroleum-powered warfare, a relatively small European nation with few natural resources and no defensible borders could not afford to pursue such fantasies. Cultural dynamics dating back to the Middle Ages, fanned into flame by the romantic nationalism of the post-Napoleonic period and wielded as a deliberate instrument of state by German politicians from 1848 on, made any open and reasoned discussion of the conflict between these injunctions a political and psychological impossibility. The result was a classic double bind, which played out in the usual manner.

Many factors contributed to the rise and disastrous career of the Nazi state. Still, it is worth noting that the behaviour of that state had remarkable similarities to the clinical phenomena of acute paranoid schizophrenia: the megalomaniac inflation of importance through ever more elaborate narratives of self-justification, the frantic quest to identify and punish scapegoats who could be blamed for all of Germany's self-created problems, the increasingly ornate edifice of jargon and catchphrases that reduced language to self-cancelling noise—all were present, serving their usual roles as the defence mechanisms of a psyche trying to impose its own arbitrary and rigid structure of meaning on a universe of experience that contradicted that meaning in every particular. Since that psyche was collective rather than individual, the consequences of the psychotic break Germany suffered in 1933 were not limited to one person's family, friends, and associates; instead, much of Europe became a madhouse in which the patients went about armed and jackbooted.

THE DOUBLE BIND OF PROGRESS

Many more examples of the collective double bind in action could be described here. The point to these reflections, however, is that the end of the age of cheap abundant fossil fuels makes a conflict of this same kind very nearly inevitable. The first injunction of the double bind imposed by peak oil is the overt and constantly verbalized insistence that progress, defined specifically in terms of those directions in which contemporary industrial society can be portrayed to have advanced in the recent past, is as inevitable as it is beneficial.

The second injunction is the covert and unspoken realization, on the part of a growing number of people in the industrial world, that the last decade or so of change resembles regression and decline far more than it does any meaningful sense of the word "progress", and that the future shows every sign of delivering much more of the same.

The third, as in the cases just cited, is provided by the emotional toll entailed in letting go of three centuries of triumphant ideology that defined the people of the world's industrial nations as the cutting edge of human history and thus excused radically unequal distributions of wealth among nations—for example, the fact that the 5 per cent of humanity that lived in the United States at the end of the twentieth century consumed a quarter of the world's energy resources and a third of its raw materials and industrial product. To question the civil religion of progress is to abandon a core source of meaning and justification in modern life, one that is heavily supported by a galaxy of influential institutions as well as by a widespread popular consensus. Turning away from so deep and pervasive an element of contemporary culture is not done lightly or without substantial personal costs.

Yet the costs of remaining within the double bind can be significantly greater and can have massive collective implications alongside their great significance to individuals. If, in fact, three centuries of rapid technological progress are coming to an end in our lifetimes, as a result of peak oil and a range of parallel conflicts between the ideology of perpetual growth and the hard limits of a finite planet, many of the choices the world's industrial societies are making today are hopelessly misguided. It is fair to say, in fact, that any society willing to face the end of an age of cheap abundant energy and technological acceleration in a reasoned way would deal with its future in a manner precisely opposite to the way we are currently dealing with ours.

Instead of extracting fossil fuels from the ground as quickly as possible in a futile attempt to keep the price of energy down, for example, a sane society would arguably take effective steps to decrease its use of fossil fuels, and thus leave them in the ground for as long as possible; letting prices rise in response to market pressures would be a logical way to foster that decrease. Instead of squandering its remaining resources and time on long-shot technological gambles to keep the illusion of progress going, in turn, such a society would be well advised to inventory its existing knowledge base and technical resources with an eye to those things that could make it possible to support humane and decent lifestyles for as many people as possible on a shrinking energy budget. Instead of pursuing change for its own sake, such a society might well choose to identify environmental, cultural, and technical factors that should be preserved intact and take active steps to preserve them. These steps and others like them might not succeed, but for a society facing a future of energy scarcity, economic contraction, and technological regression, they would certainly be wiser than the frantic efforts to maintain the fiction of business-as-usual that counts for sensible policy in the world's industrial nations today.

Yet steps of the sort just outlined are unthinkable in precisely those industrial nations that would most benefit from them. Like Dorothy Martin's followers, today's believers in the civil religion of progress are, by and large, committed to a set of beliefs that place them in unavoidable conflict with reality; however, the double bind that rises out of that very conflict places potent psychological obstacles in the path of the most reasonable response to the failure of those beliefs—discarding them, that is, in favour of beliefs and actions better suited to the world as it exists. The psychology of the progress myth all but guarantees that most industrial societies will continue to pursue technological progress long past the point of diminishing returns, while rejecting more useful options that fail to further the myth.

Given the explosive mixture of economic volatility, environmental breakdown, and social and political stress that appears to be building up around the failure of the myth of progress just now, the possibility that this profoundly unhelpful but deeply human response will be a fruitful source of disasters is hard to dismiss out of hand. That possibility is amplified by patterns of social psychology that, so far, have all but guaranteed that the available alternatives to the myth of progress are no more functional as models for the future than the myth of progress itself.

FOUR
Peak oil as deviance

Despite the social pressures and institutional incentives bolstering the civil religion of progress, not everyone in the modern industrial world is a devout believer in that faith, and even among the believers, as in other religions, there is no shortage of disputes over questions of faith and morals. Postmodern theorists have made the useful point that social mores and values are always contested phenomena, redefined variously by competing voices that always bring agendas of their own into the discussion. Most of these voices claim to speak for God, truth, the majority, or whatever other abstraction traditionally serves to anchor successful truth claims in any given debate—most voices, but not all.

Even among believers in progress, therefore, what counts as progressive in any given case is by no means a straightforward question. The imagery of progress most often found in the cultural mainstream of industrial societies is a pastiche in which technological, economic, moral, and intellectual betterment all blur together, and it is far from uncommon for the ingredients of this melange to be pried apart by competing interests and used to support or assail the claim that any given change represents progress. The ongoing debate between proponents of nuclear energy and adherents of "green energy" technologies such as wind power has this as a frequent theme, with each side in the debate striving to portray its own preferred technology as more progressive and the other side's offerings as outmoded and regressive.

Outside the realm of technology, such contentions are even more common. In today's world, it is a poor excuse for a political ideology, creative movement, cultural fashion, or marketing gimmick that cannot find some reasoning, however dubious, to support the claim that it is more progressive, more avant-garde, further out on the cutting edge than its rivals. A rich fund of unintended irony often surrounds such pronouncements, for there is surprisingly little that is genuinely new in any of these fields. Thus, for example, the latest revival of public masturbation as performance art was once again hailed as cutting-edge and avant-garde by critics who were blissfully ignorant of the fact that it has been reinvented every thirty years or so since the 1890s (Bayles, 1994).

The sheer emotional power of the concept of progress makes such embarrassments all but impossible to avoid. Central to the mythic narrative of progress is a stereotyped conflict between an inspired and innovative few, portrayed as the heroic standard-bearers of the future, and an ignorant and entrenched majority, filling the role of obscurantist defenders of the outworn past. Popular works on the history of science, culture, and the arts impose this narrative on the past even when the data have to suffer drastic distortions in the process.

Consider, for example, the insistence, still common in popular histories today, that most Europeans at the time of

Christopher Columbus believed that the world was flat, and that this was the reason that scholars dismissed Columbus' claim that Asia could be reached by sailing westwards from Europe. It has been shown repeatedly that this claim is a nineteenth-century fabrication without the least scrap of evidence to support it (Russell, 1991). Any survey of contemporary sources—for example, the *De Sphaera* of John of Sacrobosco, the standard textbook of astronomy in secondary schools across Europe in Columbus's time—demonstrates that late-medieval Europeans not only knew that the world was round but had a fairly good estimate of its correct size (Thorndyke, 1949). In addition, contemporary accounts demonstrate decisively that those who rejected Columbus's arguments did so on the grounds that Asia was too far away to be reached with the maritime technology available at the time.

Furthermore, the critics were quite correct. The only reason Columbus and his sailors did not perish miserably in the midst of empty ocean a third of the way to Asia was the presence of a wild card of which Columbus himself was completely ignorant, and the reality of which he refused to accept until his death: the unexpected appearance of two continents, previously unknown to Europeans, that happened to be in the way. The notion that Columbus's critics thought that the world was flat nonetheless remains firmly fixed in place among the credos of modern industrial culture, because the myth of progress requires that every event that we define as progressive came out of a struggle against entrenched obscurantism. Where history fails to follow that narrative, it is rewritten as required.

This is only one of many examples of the way that our collective sense of the past is held hostage by the mythic narrative of progress. The same process of rewriting imposes itself with equal force on conceptions of the present and future. The quest for commercial fusion power mentioned earlier in this book is a useful example. At this point, after more than half a century of repeated failure whose lessons no one seems willing to learn, the fusion research community is arguably a better example of entrenched obscurantism than were the careful fifteenth-century geographers who measured Columbus' proposals against the known diameter of the Earth and found them lacking (Seife, 2008). Yet fusion researchers, despite their institutional support and nearly limitless governmental backing, still like to portray themselves to the media as heroic Columbuses and thereby press their scattered and underfunded critics into service as the presumptive voices of authority and orthodoxy.

The narrative of conflict central to the mythology of progress, in other words, depends on the availability of an antagonist who has, or can be claimed to have, certain stereotyped qualities. To some extent, as already suggested, that role is filled by proponents of competing technologies, or, for that matter, competing political, artistic, or cultural movements, whose claims to represent the wave of the future pose a challenge to one another. To some extent also, as in the example of fusion just cited, anyone who criticizes a technological project on any grounds—no matter how absurd the project or how sensible the objections happen to be—can count on being drafted into the imaginary army of entrenched antagonists of progress.

There is yet another important source that helps to fill the ranks of the opposition. The civil religion of progress has its competing schools and its heresies, to be sure, but it also has its apostates—those people in modern industrial societies who reject the faith in progress outright and embrace a competing religion. Their place in the structure of the myth is one familiar to students of social psychology, and a glance into the psychology of deviance will be necessary in order to make sense of their role in the twilight years of the age of progress.

DEVIANCE AND STATUS PANIC

In the late-nineteenth and early twentieth century, when the issues surrounding social deviance first came under scientific inquiry, a simplistic model derived from earlier religious treatments of the same subject dominated the field. The literature of social pathology, as it was called in those days, assumed that certain behaviours were *ipso facto* bad for the individual and society alike, that society sensibly prohibited those behaviours, and that the question that needed solving was why individuals pursued those behaviours anyway (Mills, 1943). Researchers using that model, however, found themselves unable to explain the drastic differences in the behaviours different societies and subcultures classed as unacceptable, or, for that matter, the awkward way in which behaviours that were unacceptable and harshly punished when done by or to members of one group were ignored or even celebrated when done by or to members of another group in the same society (Lemert, 1951).

A range of new theoretical approaches emerged in the middle years of the twentieth century to deal with these complexities. While they differed significantly among themselves on most issues, the majority of these new approaches shifted the focus of inquiry away from the deviant acts that had been central to research in the social pathology era, in order to explore the ways that actions and persons are defined as deviant by the broader society. That question turned out to be crucial, not only in itself, but as a bridge to more significant and challenging questions about the roles that deviance, and deviant persons, played in the social structure and collective psychology of the society that defines them as deviant.

The core insight that followed from these latter questions is that deviance serves two essential roles for the community. First, deviance is among the most important ways that a community defines and experiences its own boundaries: we know who we are, in effect, by identifying someone else who represents to us what we are not (Coser, 1962; Dentler & Erikson, 1959; McClenon, 1984). If, as suggested by sociologist Edward Shils, social phenomena may be mapped out along a continuum extending from a centre of commonly accepted values, practices, and institutions to a periphery of deviant alternatives (Shils, 1975), it is by defining the periphery as deviant that the centre experiences itself as the centre.

Second, deviance is among the most important ways that a community prepares alternative options for itself in an uncertain world: what is today a deviant belief system or behaviour may turn out in the future to be necessary or useful to the community (Ben-Yehuda, 1985; Douglas, 1977). This second function has been used often enough in recent history that it is readily traced; consider, for example, how middle-class American women entering the workforce—a deviant practice a century ago—has become standard practice today.

The first, boundary-setting function is primary, however. It is so central to identity, collective as well as individual, that if no obvious candidates present themselves for the role of representing the not-self, someone will be dragooned into the role and made to act the part. The witch panics of late-medieval and early modern Europe are a case in point; scrambling to shore up a crumbling collective identity in the wake of the failure of the Crusades and the trauma of the Black Death, Christian Europeans invented an imaginary image of the malevolent Other, imposed it on tens of thousands of unfortunate individuals, tortured them to make them accept that identity, and then killed them for accepting it (Goode & Ben-Yehuda, 2009). The earnest officers of the Inquisition, who had detailed checklists of things that witches were supposed to do, and who tortured people accused of witchcraft until they gave the right answers to every item on the list, offer a useful reminder of how far societies will go to provide themselves with the deviants that they desire.

In the vast majority of examples, though, matters never have to be taken that far. When the punishments imposed for being defined as deviant are significantly less unpleasant than being burnt at the stake, individuals can normally be found who are willing to adopt the deviant identity as their own. Any number of reasons can lead people to embrace a role of this kind (Matza, 1969): there are those who react against a society's real or imagined faults, for instance, by taking on whatever oppositional stance the society offers them; there are those who are pressed into a deviant role by the expectations of parents, teachers, or other authority figures; there are also those whose sense of self is sufficiently weak that the thought of adopting a clearly defined identity, even a despised or condemned one, is a potent lure. Since societies need their deviants to define themselves, and to explore alternative options without committing themselves in advance, it is by no means uncommon for covert means to be found to encourage deviance and to reward deviants for their misbehaviour, or at least to provide them with a livelihood so they can afford to carry out their assigned function of defining what good citizens are not.

Just as deviants are commonly rewarded for doing the things that their society officially insists they should not do, in turn they are routinely punished for doing what their society officially insists they ought to do—that is, to give up their deviant ways. Once a person or group has been labelled as deviant, in fact, any effort by that person or group to conform to the mores of the majority will reliably evoke a sharply negative reaction in the majority itself. Sociologist C. Wright Mills described this reaction as *status panic* (Mills, 1951). Any attempt to narrow the distance that separates deviants from the majority threatens the collective sense of identity that defines the group from which the deviants are excluded, and which their exclusion itself defines. The more effectively the deviants succeed in conforming to the mores of the community that excludes them, the more drastic, in turn, the status panic will generally be, and the more violent the means by which it will be expressed.

Thus, it is anything but accidental that it was Germany—in which Jews had achieved a more thorough assimilation into gentile society than anywhere else in Europe in the late-nineteenth and early twentieth centuries—that turned on its Jewish population in a genocidal frenzy not long thereafter. In the same way, it was during the years when gay Americans kept their sexual orientation hidden and tried to pass for heterosexual that they suffered the most extreme forms of abuse by the rest of society. After the Stonewall riots of 1969, as the gay community claimed a public presence and gay individuals adopted fashions and habits that allowed their identity to be identified at a glance, the status panic that their assimilation to the mainstream had engendered among the heterosexual majority began to give way. By visibly defining themselves as different, American gays made it unnecessary for heterosexuals to raise social barriers against them, and major shifts—such as the legalization of same-sex marriage in a growing number of US states—have duly followed.

The process of defining the boundaries of the religion of progress in contemporary culture is at least as complex as any of the examples just cited, if not more so, and has involved repeated movements back and forth across the boundary between overt deviance and status panic. In his study of the social dimensions of parapsychology, for example, James McClenon has described repeated outbursts of status panic on the part of the scientific mainstream towards those branches of scientific inquiry that have been labelled deviant (McClenon, 1984). The more carefully parapsychologists tried to follow scientific norms and conform to the expectations of the scientific subculture, he showed, the more forcefully scientists in more established fields excluded and denounced them.

Behind the quarrel, and lending it much of its force, was a fierce dispute about whether the study of psychic phenomena was the next step in scientific progress, as the parapsychologists claimed, or whether it was a regression towards medieval obscurantism, as their opponents insisted. In an age in which progress is considered sacred, such claims and counterclaims are a potent tool for exercising influence and claiming positions of privilege. Since the glorious future towards which progress is advancing remains forever undefined, in turn there is no objective way to settle disputes of this kind, and whatever decision a community renders in such cases always has much more to teach about the distribution of authority and influence in the community than it does about the issues over which the quarrel has apparently been fought.

SHADOW AND SCAPEGOAT

The sociological explorations and redefinitions of deviance just described did not take place in an intellectual vacuum. They paralleled, and were doubtless influenced by, the slightly earlier work of depth psychologists, who explored the same phenomena on the level of the individual personality. The core insight of Freud and his followers—the existence of an unconscious level of the mind, capable of influencing consciousness in the service of its own autonomous motives—succeeded, among its other achievements, in casting light on many of the psychological processes by which individuals accept, reject, evade, and manipulate the behavioural norms of their societies.

Freud's classic tripartite model of the psyche was, in fact, largely defined by the psychological issues that surround the ego's relation to social norms. The uncontrolled desires and fantasies of the id, which are the raw material of deviance, and the rules of the superego, which are the personal reflection of the collective identity of society, mirror the relation of periphery to centre described by Shils; they form the continuum along which the ego seeks its point of balance. Deviance, from a Freudian standpoint, is thus the triumph of the id over the superego. It may be deliberately embraced by the ego in an act of rebellion against the superego, but more often it takes a subtler and potentially more dangerous form.

Those desires of the id that the ego is unwilling to allow into consciousness, according to Freud, fill a role in the structure of the psyche similar to the role filled by deviants in a society, and they are pushed out beyond the limits of consciousness in much the same way that deviants are pushed out beyond the limits of social acceptance. Just as deviants are inevitably part of the whole system of the society, in turn repressed desires inevitably become part of the structure of the psyche in a "return of the repressed" that can twist the entire architecture of the self into various forms of neurotic dysfunction.

The Freudian model of deviance has proven useful in understanding and treating many kinds of neurotic behaviour. Still, Jung's revision of the model has proven more fruitful as a tool for making sense of the tangled relationship of the self to social norms. That revision centres on the archetype of the shadow. In Jungian theory, this is an autonomous structure of the collective unconscious that serves as a catchall for every part of the individual's identity and behaviour that the individual him/herself is unable or unwilling to accept. The shadow is to the ego, in this formulation, exactly what the deviant is to the larger society: like society, the ego defines what it is by rejecting what it is not—or, more precisely, what it believes it is not.

The link between shadow and deviance is not simply a parallelism, however, because archetypes express—or, in Jung's term, constellate—themselves in experience whenever conditions permit, and the most common way for an archetype to constellate itself for the unsophisticated ego is by projection onto another person. This may well be the core function of archetypes, since the archetypes themselves, according to Jungian theory, are the psychic expressions of that which biologists understand as instinct (Jacobi, 1959). Each normal infant thus comes into the world with a nascent psyche in which the abstract mother-imago, the archetype of the mother, is the dominant factor, and any person who responds to the infant in a maternal way becomes, to extend the metaphor implicit in Jung's phrasing, a screen onto which the archetype is projected.

In the same way, the archetype of the child, the abstract infant-imago, is a living and potent presence in the psyche of most women; the girl playing with her doll is cultivating the art of projecting that archetype appropriately. She may grow up to bear children of her own, in which case each child in turn will become the screen onto which the infant-imago is projected, or she may not, in which case the archetype may be projected elsewhere: onto someone else's child, a pet, a spouse, the infant Jesus, or some other focus. Similar patterns relate individuals in other ways; when two people fall in love, far more often than not each has projected the lover-imago onto the other and is seeing only the archetypal image—a process that may help explain the noticeable gap that so often distinguishes the lover's opinion of the beloved's charms from any more objective assessment.

The archetype of the shadow, in all probability, has a similar origin in instinctual patterns inherited from the archaic, prehuman past. The shadow is the enemy-imago, the archetype of whatever has to be defeated and destroyed in order for the ego to survive: the rival for love or power, the foe at the gate, the predator lying in wait in the wilderness. It differs from the other archetypes in two crucial ways. The first, obviously enough, is its emotional tone. The other archetypes in their normal expressions stimulate and are stimulated by various forms of love and desire, but the shadow stimulates and is stimulated by hatred and fear.

The second difference is subtler and unfolds from the complexities of ego development in a species that has overlaid these straightforward instinctual patterns of relationship with a plethora of culturally specific complexities. Since the shadow archetype tends to constellate around anything that rouses feelings of hatred and fear, it is by no means uncommon for a child taught to reject some part of his or her own personality—say, sexual desires in a sexually repressive culture, or a desire for autonomy in a culture that demands obedience—to have the shadow archetype constellate around the rejected trait.

For the child to accept the trait as part of its ego thereafter would bring unbearable inner conflict, since this would define the ego itself as its own enemy, to be hated and feared by itself. The child usually responds by projecting the shadow-identified traits of its own ego outward onto some other person or group of people. This is an uncomfortable expedient at best, and it has to be repeated frequently to keep up the illusion that the hated and feared traits only belong to the other people who are bad and wrong. The structure of the Batesonian double bind is relevant here: the projection of the shadow-content onto another person serves as the first injunction, the suppressed recognition that the shadow-content is part of one's own identity as the second, and the painful emotional cost of owning up to the shadow-content as the third.

It is a commonplace of Jungian therapy that whatever a patient finds most intolerable in other people is certain to be a core part of his or her own shadow. Still, the point relevant to the present discussion is that this process is central to the social psychology of deviance. A deviant, in this sense, is someone onto whom a great many people have agreed to project some or all of the shadow archetype as this is constellated in their psyches, thus relieving the strain involved in recognizing the shadow in themselves.

Whether or not the deviant has any objective resemblance to the constellated shadow figure varies from case to case. Sometimes people can be found who actually possess the traits the society wishes to project upon its deviants: the street gangs and organized criminals of the United States, whose actions match up fairly well to the violent amorality that corresponds to the portion of the American shadow they are expected to carry, are one example on this end of the spectrum. In other cases, those assigned to carry the shadow may have nothing at all in common with the traits assigned them: the victims of the late-medieval witch hunts mentioned earlier are a good example.

The processes by which individuals are selected and groomed for deviant status, and provided with incentives of various kinds to play the deviant part selected for them, have been studied extensively in the context of family relationships (Minuchin, 1974; Perera, 1986). One or more children in a troubled family may be assigned the role of "black sheep" and covertly encouraged to act out a disruptive role in the family, either to provide one or both parents with a justification for acting out some other role (for example, punitive enforcer of proper conduct), to redirect the focus of the family's attention away from some unmentionable issue (for example, a parent's drinking problem), or to serve in some other way to prop up the often rickety narratives by which a dysfunctional family defines itself.

Very often the parents and "good" children—that is, those children who have been assigned this role in the family drama—will overtly criticize the "bad" child or children for acting out the role they have been assigned, while at the same time covertly rewarding behaviour that enacts the role and punishing behaviour that conflicts with it. The rewards and punishments vary from family to family, but fairly often the simple act of granting and withholding attention is a central element. If a child can only count on receiving the parental attention it needs and craves by acting out a disruptive role, then it will reliably act out that role.

THE LOYAL OPPOSITION

The same process can be traced in the emergence of those forms of deviance that act out shadow roles in the narratives of a troubled society, instead of those of a troubled family. The craving for attention from the community can be as powerful a force as the equivalent desire in the family setting, and it is often by granting and withholding attention that the spokespersons of the community recruit and discipline the deviants through whom the community defines its own identity. These latter become, to borrow and recycle a political cliché, the loyal opposition—loyal, in this case, to the community whose mores they seemingly reject but whose needs for definition of identity they faithfully fulfil. Those persons who fill the approved deviant roles in the narrative, and thus allow themselves to be used as a target for the projection of the collective shadow, are therefore made the centre of public attention, while those who deviate in other ways are ignored.

This pattern is particularly easy to trace out in relation to the mythic narrative of progress. The narrative, as already mentioned, requires an assortment of individuals to play the role of defenders of the superstitious and obscurantist past, so that the proponents of whatever happens to be defined as progress at any given time can act out their own assigned role of heroic innovators overthrowing the dead weight of dogma and orthodoxy. Advocates of competing versions of progress make up one pool of potential candidates for the losing role, to be sure, and so do any group of people who object to some change proposed as progress, no matter how reasonable and appropriate their objections may happen to be. It is more useful still to have defenders of dogmatic obscurantism who actually play the part. These are provided by an assortment of deviant subcultures in contemporary industrial societies who, like "black sheep" children in a dysfunctional family, are covertly rewarded and encouraged for playing the deviant role that society assigns them.

Fundamentalist religious sects make up the largest single group of these subcultures in the modern industrial world. It is rarely noticed nowadays just how recent the fundamentalist movement is in Christianity and how decisively it has broken with the rest of Christian history (Boyer, 1992). The emergence of fundamentalism in Christianity happened at the same time as, and proceeded in parallel with, the rise of scientific materialism and atheism in the Western world; the spread of fundamentalism to other faiths—for example, Judaism, Islam, Hinduism—has similarly moved in lockstep with the spread of scientific materialism and atheism to other parts of the world. While it is doubtless controversial to suggest that fundamentalism represents the largely unconscious embrace, by religious people, of an image of religion that was invented and promoted by opponents of religion, there are aspects of fundamentalism that are difficult to explain in any other way.

The issues that have become central to contemporary fundamentalist discourse, for example, are far more relevant to the civil religion of progress than they are to the religious traditions from which fundamentalism arises. Darwinian evolution actually has little if anything to say, for example, to the core of the Christian religion. A narrowly literal interpretation of the Book of Genesis is nowhere demanded by any of the historic creeds of the Christian church, and Christian tradition includes a wealth of alternative ways of interpreting Biblical texts, many of which would allow a Darwinian view of natural history to coexist comfortably with Christian faith. Why, then, has the rejection of evolution in favour of a dubiously scriptural "creation science" become so important a credo among today's Christian fundamentalists?

The same question could be asked concerning many other hot-button issues of contemporary fundamentalism, Christian and otherwise, which have little if any relevance to what used to be recognized as the essential beliefs of the faith traditions in question. Complex forces have no doubt worked together to remake these religious movements in so odd a way, but social pressures on fundamentalists to conform to an image of religion that plays an adversarial role in the myth of progress have, I suggest, played a crucial role in that transformation.

Fundamentalist Christianity is by no means the only recent social movement that has been thoroughly reshaped in this manner. The New Age movement offers a particularly clear view of the process at work (Hanegraaff, 1996). In the 1970s, when it emerged out of a complicated blend of 1960s popular mysticism, such earlier alternative spiritual movements as New Thought, and a variety of avant-garde movements in the sciences, the New Age movement not only embraced the mythology of progress but promoted its own claim to the prized status of a uniquely progressive phenomenon (Ferguson, 1980).

As the movement matured, however, the pressure to conform with the wider society's model of acceptable deviance came into play. New Age groups, in response to this pressure, cut their ties with the scientific community and with avant-garde cultural movements such as environmentalism, replaced them with a suite of well-aged ideas from such sources as Spiritualism and Theosophy, and redefined themselves with increasing exactness to fit public expectations concerning fringe spirituality. At this point, as a result, there is little new about the New Age, and arguably even less of the original inspiration that set the movement on its way. Instead, the New Age has come to fill the function of a stage property for narratives enacted by a more successful claimant for the hero's role in the myth of progress—the scientific community—which, to maintain its hold on that role, needs a steady supply of opponents.

Yet another contemporary social movement that has come to fill the same role is environmentalism. Like religious fundamentalism and the New Age community, the environmental movement started off with a distinctive agenda of its own, one that in some ways was more threatening to the religion of progress than either of the movements just named. As it emerged from the counterculture of the late 1960s, the environmental movement embodied an overt critique of the concept of progress and a willingness to lead by example, embracing unpopular lifestyle changes and tapping into a range of inchoate but widely felt dissatisfactions with industrial society.

At a time when several rivers in America's industrial heartland were so heavily polluted that they routinely caught fire on hot summer days, the environmentalist critique was hard to dismiss out of hand, and ideas derived from the movement found wide acceptance For a time it became possible, and even fashionable, for intellectuals in many industrial societies to challenge the civil religion of progress outright (e.g., Roszak, 1972) and to propose that any further progress along the lines then envisioned would lead not to Utopia but to disaster (e.g., Meadows, Meadows, Randers, & Behrens, 1972). As young people in many parts of the industrial world embraced such ideas, it seemed possible that the church of progress had met its Protestant reformation. From another perspective, this was an example of the second function of deviance mentioned above: the environmental movement had traced out a set of options that turned out to have much to offer society as a whole.

Yet the religion of progress proved to be more durable than the environmental insurgency, and it soon returned environmentalism to its earlier status as a deviant movement. Before long, the same processes of redefinition already seen in the fundamentalist and New Age movements came into play. Environmental groups and individual activists who abandoned the critique of progress, gave up alternative lifestyles in favour of full participation in the consumer society, and pursued relatively ineffective means of seeking their goals, received favourable media attention, ample funding, and access to political influence as a junior partner in parties towards the liberal end of the spectrum. Those who refused to do so were quickly marginalized, not only by the wider society, but by more compliant environmentalists as well.

All this took place alongside the shifts in collective mood and behaviour, away from conservation and an environmental ethic and towards conspicuous consumption and ecological neglect, discussed in the first chapter of this book. Actions in the political sphere helped drive those shifts. Governments in much of the industrial world supported conservation programmes in the 1970s, in response to the energy crises of that decade, and then swung around and supported consumption in the 1980s, in response to the slowing of the economy at the beginning of that decade. This abrupt shift in social mores meant that people who had adopted approved beliefs and actions in the 1970s suddenly found themselves encouraged by governments and the media to embrace what, during the decade just ended, had been assigned the status of deviant beliefs and actions by the same governments and media. It is hardly surprising that so many people in the 1980s adopted self-consciously antisocial attitudes of the "Greed is good" variety. Having been encouraged by authoritative figures to adopt what they had been taught to see as a deviant identity, they embraced it as fully as they knew how.

In recent decades, as a result of these changes, environmental activism has had very few successes, and its function has become the standard deviant role of our time—that is, to oppose the heroic march of progress, and fail. Meanwhile the issues around which the environmental movement originally coalesced have not gone away, and a good many of them have worsened significantly. The fact that most environmental activism has been redirected to become a source of support for the existing order of society has not changed the nature, or the importance, of the issues that environmental activists think they are addressing.

PROGRESS AND APOCALYPSE

To a significant extent, then, apostates from the civil religion of progress have been fitted, by processes familiar to social psychologists, into roles and behaviours defined for them by the cultural mainstream. Yet it is important to remember that those whose job it is to fail need some justification for continuing their efforts in the face of repeated failure, and this typically takes the role of a narrative that frames their struggles in a supportive manner. It so happens that a single counter-narrative, opposing the narrative of progress, is shared by all three of the movements just named, and also by most other movements that have been assigned the social role of opposing progress. This counter-narrative is the narrative of apocalypse: the belief that progress will not continue indefinitely into the future but is, instead, on the brink of a sudden cataclysmic end.

A complex history lies behind the conflict between the narratives of progress and apocalypse, for the myth of progress itself is derived in large part from older apocalyptic traditions rooted in the religious heritage of the West. The Christian vision of the End of Days, which crystallized in the early Middle Ages around the vivid imagery of the Book of Revelation, embraced two contrasting themes—on the one hand, the descent of the world into chaos and mass death at the hands of the Antichrist; on the other, the miraculous renewal of the world following the Second Coming, after which all sorrow and sin would be banished forever. The tension between those themes provides much of the compelling narrative power of Christian apocalyptic myth, but in a great many visions of the future derived from the Christian narrative, that tension proved too great to bear.

Sociologist Philip Lamy has argued that in modern times, accordingly, the rich complexity of Christian apocalyptic myth has been splintered into "fractured apocalypses" that edit and rearrange the themes of the original story to suit contemporary social needs (Lamy, 1998). The myth of progress is among the oldest and most widely accepted of these fragments of Revelation. In the myth of progress, the Second Coming has already happened, in the form of the scientific revolution of the seventeenth and eighteenth centuries; the kingdom of Antichrist has accordingly been projected back onto the prescientific past, when people allegedly believed the world was flat, and opponents of progress fill the role of minions of an already defeated Antichrist who still obstinately refuse to give up the fight. Ahead lies the Millennium of perpetual progress, with the dream of the superlatively technological society of the future hanging in the air like the New Jerusalem of the last chapters of the Book of Revelation.

The social movements that provide opposition to the followers of this faith, in turn, have their own fractured apocalypses. Each of these stands in opposition to the mythic narrative of progress, but each does so in a different way.

Christian fundamentalism, in the course of its evolution, has come to embrace an End Times doctrine that draws its imagery from the Book of Revelation but involves radical redefinitions of older Christian apocalyptic beliefs (Boyer, 1992). To today's fundamentalists, history's arrow proceeds in a straight line towards the closest possible approximation of hell on earth, and it has nearly completed that trajectory. What the unbelieving world defines as progress, the fundamentalist believer sees as regress, an accelerating descent into a world gone mad, in which the righteous remnant has only one hope: the Rapture, a miraculous intervention by God himself that will teleport every believing Christian to safety in heaven. Here below, once the Rapture happens, all hell will quite literally break loose, and the sinful majority of human beings will be annihilated by a seven-year crescendo of plagues and other cataclysms, recounted in gruesome and gloating detail in contemporary Christian apocalyptic literature. Only after all the unbelievers are slaughtered will the

Second Coming occur and the earth, cleansed of sin, be fit for Christian habitation.

The New Age movement has its own rich apocalyptic tradition, which does not rely on imagery from a single sacred text and therefore has taken on a much greater diversity of forms than the fundamentalist Christian version. The genocidal fury that pervades the fundamentalist vision, to be sure, is rarely present in New Age apocalypses. Instead, the core of the great change that most New Age believers expect in the near future could be summed up, without too much inaccuracy, as "I told you so". Whether UFOs from an advanced galactic civilization land on the White House lawn, or a sudden leap of consciousness transforms the thinking of humanity, or some other miraculous event occurs—and there is no shortage of competing accounts of the nature of that long-awaited event—the message New Age believers expect it to proclaim to the world is that they are right and all their critics are wrong. The scientists and sceptics who thought of themselves as the proponents of progress will be revealed as the defenders of obscurantism and ignorance, while the New Age teachings that these persons condemned will turn out to reveal the true route of progress along which humanity must advance towards whatever shining destiny it might happen to be assigned.

The environmental movement, for its part, puts its faith in a far simpler apocalyptic narrative: unless we stop maltreating the environment, the earth will die and so will we. Since this narrative does not depend on supernatural forces for its fulfilment, and a significant body of scientific research offers at least qualified support to its claims, the environmental apocalypse is less easily dismissed by the cultural mainstream than are the others, and it has accordingly been put to use tolerably often in recent years as a debating point by one or another political faction in its strivings for power.

Its relationship to the myth of progress is also more complex than those of the two apocalyptic traditions just discussed. While the apocalyptic dimension of environmentalism began, in the early days of the environmental movement, as a direct challenge to the myth of progress, shifts since then have given rise to strange hybrids. All through the shrill rhetoric on both sides of recent debates about anthropogenic climate change, for example, runs a curious note of triumphalism. The advocates of climate activism are effectively arguing that humanity, as a result of the march of progress, has become so powerful that it can destroy the earth itself, while their opponents insist that if anything goes wrong, humanity is powerful enough to fix it. Both sides of the argument thus amount to a glorification of progress

This may go a long way to explain why worrying about anthropogenic climate change is an acceptable form of deviance in contemporary industrial society, receiving ample attention from the mainstream media, while concern about peak oil is largely excluded from the collective discourse of our time. The narrative of anthropogenic climate change, at bottom, is a story about human power and is thus congenial to believers in the myth of progress. The narrative of peak oil, by contrast, is a story about human limits. Since it argues that what we have called progress was made possible by fossil fuels, and will go away as the ability to extract fossil fuels declines to zero, the peak oil narrative is utterly uncongenial to believers in the myth of progress, and the cognitive dissonance between the hard facts of peak oil and the whole suite of beliefs about the world centred on progress is strong enough that the facts are all but guaranteed to be ignored.

The apocalyptic traditions of fundamentalism, the New Age movement, and environmentalism, however, have an additional feature that is crucial to their current role as a support for the competing narrative of progress. In each of these narratives, it is essential to the outcome of the story that the defenders of truth should fail in their efforts. The Rapture and the Second Coming will only arrive when, despite all the efforts of good Christians, the world has plunged into the nethermost pit of wickedness; the great leap of consciousness that New Age believers await is only necessary because, at the end of the day, the process of trying to convince the world to accept New Age teachings by any less miraculous means has failed. The environmental apocalypse, in turn, is precisely what will happen if the world does not listen to warnings of imminent doom—and the growing fixation on a prophetic role of this kind is a subtle but effective way of encouraging environmental activists to express their warnings of imminent doom in such a way that, in fact, the world will not listen.

In all three cases, the more deeply believers commit themselves to an apocalyptic worldview, the less incentive they have to take actions that might succeed in changing the world as it is, since any day now, according to the belief, the apocalypse will arrive and make all such actions superfluous. Thus, believers in all three deviant traditions have a strong incentive to fulfil the role that the narrative of progress assigns them, and they also have a range of plausible excuses for continuing to embrace and foster the existing order of things in their own lives—for example, to engage in behaviours that a stricter analysis would consider sinful, unenlightened, or ecologically harmful, depending on the belief system in question—since the imminence of the apocalypse makes the coherence of individual behaviour with ideology an unimportant issue.

And peak oil? Here the division already noted between the nature of activism and the nature of the issues activists think they are addressing is of central importance. Peak oil activism has only existed in any organized form since the very late 1990s, and only became a matter of broader public awareness in 2005, when the publication of James Howard Kunstler's best-selling *The Long Emergency* brought the challenge of peak oil to the attention of those outside the then-small peak oil subculture. Since that time, the same social pressures that reduced the environmental movement to its current state of relative impotence have been applied with equal force to peak oil activists. Given another decade or two of uninterrupted economic growth and technological advance, it would be surprising if peak oil activism were not transformed into yet another source of opponents over which progress can triumph.

The one confounding factor in this case is that we are unlikely to get another decade or two of economic growth and technological advance. The fact of peak oil poses an unavoidable challenge both to the myth of progress and to its apocalyptic pseudo-alternatives. In place of the endless upward trajectory promised by the myth of progress, or the cataclysmic sudden stop predicted by the myth of apocalypse, the implications of peak oil suggest that modern industrial civilization, like the oilfields that made it possible, has finished its long rise and will now gradually decline to something like the condition from which it began. A future defined in those terms is as unthinkable to most opponents of the myth of progress as it is to the myth's defenders—and yet this is the future taking shape around us today.

FIVE
The five stages of peak oil

All the factors discussed in previous chapters—the psychological power of the myth of progress as the foundation of the most popular civil religion of our time; the psychology of previous investment that makes straightforward discussion of the myth of progress so difficult for most people in the industrial world; the social creation of subcultures of deviance that effectively support the social norms their members believe they are opposing—make it an immense challenge to see past the stereotyped imagery of the future presented by contemporary industrial society and grasp the shape of the world towards which peak oil is driving us. Like the social crises described in the first chapter of this book, peak oil is a "problem that has no name", a source of extensive and growing difficulties, across a broad spectrum of individual and collective activities, that very few people are willing to trace back to their actual cause.

Throughout the industrial world, since the peaking of world conventional petroleum production in 2005, the boom-times of the previous decade have given way to intractable economic troubles for which no solutions seem to be forthcoming. Central bankers who boasted of their ability to rein in the business cycle and maintain a favourable environment for economic expansion found their ability to manage turmoil suddenly running into unexpected limits; political authorities have been left flailing as national economies stumble from one crisis to another. Federal Reserve Board chairman Ben Bernanke spoke for a great many others in authority when he confessed to a US Senate committee in 2008 that tools that central bankers had been using successfully for decades had suddenly stopped working.

The economic crisis that burst over the industrial world in 2008, and shows no signs of letting up as these words are being written, was fed by many factors, and a wide selection of these have been duly pilloried in the media. A remarkably casual attitude towards ethics among many of the world's largest banks has certainly been a factor; so has the widespread political habit of buying votes with expensive entitlement programmes, neglecting to raise taxes to cover them, and counting on government borrowing to make up the difference; so was the impact of the most recent speculative frenzy in the global economy, the gargantuan global real-estate bubble of 2005–2008, and the crash that followed it. It bears recalling, however, that none of these factors is new. Dishonest banking is as old as banking itself; buying votes with promises of government largesse has been a common practice for centuries; and, since the Dutch tulip bubble of 1636–1637, it has been rare for a decade to go by without at least one significant speculative boom and bust.

The question that has rarely been asked since 2008, and needs to be asked, is why events of a kind that normally produce ordinary recessions have spawned something so much more serious, protracted, and resistant to solutions this time around. A glance at the business pages of any newspaper of record will show conditions that are nearly unparalleled in living memory. Several European nations have plunged in a few years from prosperity to a level of economic crisis in which a third or more of the labour force has no jobs and the national government is struggling to avoid defaulting on its debt. In the United States, cities are declaring bankruptcy and laying off their fire-fighters and police forces, while state governments are tearing up thousands of miles of paved roads and replacing the paving with gravel, because they can no longer afford the cost of annual maintenance. These are not the signs of an ordinary downturn in the business cycle.

Bring peak oil into the picture and the severity of the crisis is easily explained. Despite immense efforts to bring new oil sources on line, global production of petroleum has been stuck on a plateau since 2004, while the potential demand for oil products has continued to rise. This has driven the price of oil to levels that were unthinkable not that many years ago. All those nations that lack significant petroleum reserves of their own have thus had to pay the equivalent of a steep tax on every form of economic activity that uses petroleum products, which in a modern industrial economy amounts to every form of economic activity without exception. It will come as no surprise that those European nations that were hit first and hardest by the Eurozone crisis that followed the 2008 crash—Portugal, Italy, Ireland, Greece, Spain—were those that were most dependent on imported petroleum.

Those nations that have petroleum reserves face a less direct but equally challenging problem. The development of oil reserves inevitably starts with those that are easiest to find and cheapest to extract, for obvious and compelling economic reasons. This means, however, that the longer a nation has been extracting oil from its territory, the more expensive it will be on average to find and develop new oilfields. Rising oil prices make such projects economically feasible, and national dependence on oil revenues often make them necessary. Still, the rising cost of oil production is not simply an abstraction; it represents additional labour, materials, goods, services, and energy needed to extract oil from more challenging geological formations.

Thus, in a nation with oil reserves, a greater fraction of the nation's total output of goods and services must be used to extract the same amount of oil. In theory, countries that produce oil for export can pass on these additional costs to their customers; in practice, when the price of oil rises too high, the global economy tips into crisis, and demand for petroleum products drops as consumers struggle to pay their energy bills. The result is a "wealth crunch" that spreads through every corner of the global economy: everything from investment capital to skilled labour to spare parts is funnelled preferentially into petroleum extraction, at the expense of all other economic sectors. The rising share of the global economy devoted to getting oil out of the ground yields flat or declining returns in terms of barrels of oil produced, while every other part of the economy is starved and suffers accordingly.

None of this is speculative, or particularly new. Economist E. F. Schumacher outlined the central importance of fossil fuel extraction to the global economy in a widely read book decades ago (Schumacher, 1973), and the burden placed by peak oil on the global economy has been analysed in detail in a variety of more recent studies (e.g., Greer, 2011a). As long as peak oil remains an unmentionable issue, though, it will be impossible for economists or anyone else to factor the rising costs of peak oil into their forecasts—and until this is done, attempts to remedy the current economic mess will almost certainly fail.

GRIEVING FOR THE FUTURE

The factors discussed in earlier chapters make it extremely difficult for most people in today's industrial world to get past the barriers that stand in the way of a frank discussion of peak oil and its impact on our future. Yet the rise of a small but significant subculture of people who are aware of peak oil, and are taking it into account in their own decisions concerning the future, is evidence that these barriers are not insurmountable. Understanding the ways that people have already come to terms with the end of progress and the failure of its promises is thus critically important, in that the paths these pioneers have taken may be the best available guide to the route that others must follow in their own time.

Information on the ways that members of the current peak oil community learned about the concept of peak oil and came to terms with its reality is sparse and, so far, almost entirely anecdotal. It may be significant, though, that one way of discussing the transition towards peak oil acceptance has entered into common use across much of the peak oil scene. This is the well-known sequence of five stages of grief—denial, anger, bargaining, depression, acceptance—introduced in a very different context by the thanatologist Elisabeth Kübler-Ross (Kübler-Ross, 1969).

In its original form, Kübler-Ross' sequence described schematically the stages through which terminally ill patients she had observed tended to pass in the course of coming to terms with their diagnosis and the imminence of their own mortality. Her later work, along with that of many other authors, applied it more broadly to the experience of grief in general (Kübler-Ross & Kessler, 2005). Kübler-Ross herself noted that not every patient passed through every stage, that some went through the stages in different orders or repeated one or more stages, and her application of the stage theory to other kinds of grief was far from doctrinaire. These virtues, unfortunately, did not survive long at the hands of popularizers who turned the five stages into an American cultural icon and used it to launch a large and lucrative industry of grief counselling at the hands of often poorly trained lay counsellors (Konigsberg, 2011).

Kübler-Ross' work, and in particular the five-stage model, have accordingly come in for extensive critique (Schultz & Alderman, 1974; Maciejewski, Zhang, Block, & Prigerson, 2007). The claim that the five stages are the inevitable, or even the optimal, model for the grieving process has been a major target of these critiques, and appropriately so. The widespread acceptance of the model in popular culture, however, suggests that it does have some value as a very general taxonomy, descriptive rather than prescriptive, of the experiences through which many people pass in the course of coming to terms with severe loss.

Certainly this is the sense in which the five stages have entered into the folklore of the contemporary peak oil community. The few therapists at present who have begun to offer counselling to those struggling with the psychological challenges of peak oil do not, to my knowledge, insist that their clients go through the five stages in order. At the same time, a casual reference to one or more of the stages in a post on a peak oil blog or a talk at a peak oil conference will get instant recognition and understanding.

It is easy to understand why this should be the case. In his essay "Mourning and Melancholia" (1917), Freud proposed that the central challenge of grief is the struggle of the ego to decathect the libidinal drive from the person who has died—a modern psychologist might describe the same process in terms of releasing an emotional investment, and the ordinary person as loosening the attachment to that person. The emotional turmoil brought by grief is the outward sign of that inward struggle, and it ceases when the ego has finished coming to terms with the loss and is ready to invest emotional energy in new relationships.

Any religious mythology defines a set of relationships that can be fully as important to the ego as its relationships with other living persons and can be the focus of emotional investments as significant as any. A devout Christian's relationship with Jesus, for example, may well be more important in his emotional life than any relationship he has with any person outside the realm of theology, and the narratives of the Bible may be more central to his understanding of the world than any other narrative structure. To lose such relationships and such frameworks of meaning can easily have an emotional impact equivalent to facing one's own imminent death—all the more so in this case, since it is precisely death that Christian faith claims to overcome. Still, as discussed in Chapter Three, believers in supernatural religions such as Christianity rarely have to face such a prospect; their kingdom, to quote Jesus, is not of this world.

That security is not shared by civil religions such as the contemporary faith in progress. Their kingdom is emphatically of this world; they survive and expand so long as they are able to provide a satisfying and meaningful explanation for the experiences of their believers. If they fail to do so now and again, the psychological mechanisms described earlier in this book make it easy for believers to ignore these failures and put their trust in the belief that successes in the past will be replicated, for them, in the future. It is when the narratives of a civil religion consistently fail to make sense of the world over an extended period that cognitive dissonance sets in. Sooner or later—though this can be delayed for a very long time—the psychological defences of belief fail also, and most of the former believers desert their discredited faith.

The failure of the civil religion of progress promises to trigger this reaction on a grand scale. Like any other civil religion, belief in the inevitability and beneficence of progress draws its strength from an unstable mixture of hagiography labelled as history, on the one hand, and contemporary experience interpreted through the eyes of faith, on the other. Narratives of the triumph of visionary apostles of progress over the forces of dogma and superstition, of the sort discussed in the previous chapter, provide the hagiography, while an endless drumbeat of books and media programmes that contrast current conditions with the supposed squalor and misery of the pre-industrial past keep the eyes of faith focused tightly on those elements of contemporary life that appear to support the prophecies of the religion of progress. Comparable measures can be found in all other religions, supernatural as well as civil, as these are core means by which faiths of all kinds preserve and propagate themselves.

The great difficulty faced by civil religions in this regard, as already discussed, is that their creeds are subject to empirical disproof. No matter how frantically Communist societies revisited the glories of the Revolution and reinterpreted the present to justify the fine details of Marxist theory, to return to an example already used, the widening gap between that theory and the everyday reality of life in a Communist nation eventually became impossible to ignore. The civil religion of progress faces a comparable crisis. As the impact of peak oil and other forms of resource depletion on the world's industrial economies continues and deepens, a growing number of people will find it impossible to square the implicit promise of endless betterment offered by faith in progress with the everyday realities of life in a society experiencing ongoing economic contraction and technological regress.

The cognitive dissonance between the belief in progress and the experience of regress will thus no doubt result in some remarkable irrationalities—and, indeed, a case could be made that it has already done so, on the collective as well as the individual scales. It may result in a level of psychological stress capable of forcing a psychotic break on the individual or collective scale. In the broadest sense, though, these are delaying tactics or, if unusually successful, dead ends. Eventually, as the myth of progress disproves itself, the great majority of people will be forced to abandon their belief in that myth and pass through a grieving process for a narrative that gave meaning to their lives, and for the glorious future of perpetual progress that will never be.

THE FIVE STAGES OF PEAK OIL

As they make that difficult journey, they will be following a path that has already been traced out by members of the contemporary peak oil community who have abandoned the same religious belief in progress and have come to terms with a future of decline and regression. That route leads to a destination that is currently classed as deviant by most people in the industrial world, but, as discussed earlier, this is hardly the first time that a deviant community on the periphery has blazed a trail that the centre would eventually have to follow.

To my knowledge, no studies have yet been carried out to determine just how people who currently accept the reality of peak oil came to that acceptance. The Kübler-Ross theory of five stages of grief, despite its relatively wide acceptance in the peak oil community itself, is at best a very rough schematization of a complex process. Still, attitudes corresponding to each of the five stages are readily encountered in discussions online on peak oil forums, and in person at peak oil conferences. It would be inappropriate to treat the five stages as more than a general taxonomy of psychological states experienced, in various sequences, by many people in the process of coping with peak oil; understood in these terms, however, it has some value.

The way these five stages express themselves in the case of peak oil may be a little clearer if it is remembered that the myth of progress is, above all else, a narrative about human agency. From within the world as it is constellated by the myth, all other forces and features of the universe are seen as ultimately subject to the human will, which may be baulked over the short term and in specific contexts, but must inevitably triumph over every obstacle in the end. That sense of the omnipotence of human agency is precisely what the fact of peak oil challenges most directly. The five stages trace out the process by which the former believer slowly relinquishes the vicarious participation in omnipotence that plays such a central role in the emotional economy of the myth of progress.

The following general descriptions thus outline the five stages of peak oil. They are based on the present author's own experiences in the peak oil community over nearly a decade and a half, and they should be taken solely as a first and unavoidably personal view of a set of patterns that deserve much more study, analysis, and assessment.

Denial

The first stage, denial, needs to be differentiated from the more casual disbelief and dismissal with which most people in any society respond to any statement that contradicts that society's central beliefs, values, and mythic narratives. What many people in the peak oil community describe as the "I'm sure they'll come up with something" attitude towards petroleum depletion—these specific words are very often used to express the attitude in question—is not denial in Kübler-Ross's sense of the term, since those who dismiss the issue have no personal stake in the dismissal; for them, the concept of peak oil simply violates industrial society's basic assumptions about reality, and therefore is brushed aside.

Denial, properly speaking, is a product of cognitive dissonance. In Kübler-Ross's original description (Kübler-Ross, 1969), which focused on the experience of people with fatal illnesses, it was the most common initial response to receiving a terminal diagnosis, and it traced out the fault line between the ego's implicit confidence in its own continued survival and the unwelcome news of impending death. Denial is a defence against the unacceptable, but it is rarely a permanent defence; rather, it buys time for the ego to come to terms with a challenge it can neither immediately accept nor permanently evade. The challenge in the case of peak oil is the end of the sense of vicarious omnipotence that the myth of progress offers, and the role of denial here is simply that of reaffirming the power of human agency to overcome the obstacle of peak oil as, according to the myth of progress, it has overcome so many other obstacles before.

Peak oil denial thus most often takes the form of an insistence that peak oil either will not happen or does not matter, and very often it leads into a vigorous search for evidence that can be used to back up one or both of these claims. Many of the arguments marshalled in support of denial are highly stereotyped—for example, the claim that whatever large oil discovery has most recently made news proves that ample oil supplies can be found for the indefinite future, or a variety of arguments about the supposed ability of alternative energy resources to replace petroleum—although this may be a consequence of the ready availability of websites that offer these specific arguments, rather than a characteristic of the denial stage as such. In the same way, the belligerent attitude so often encountered in peak oil denial may simply be a product of the Internet's culture of confrontation, rather than a sign of the imminence of the next stage. Whatever the cause, though, the bellicose insistence that peak oil is simply a theory, rather than the logical consequence of the fact that we live on a finite planet, and that it has been disproved by some set of stereotyped assertions that may have little relation to the world of fact, are typical of this stage.

Anger

With the anger stage the initial shock has passed off, so that the ego is able to begin the process of confronting the reality of its loss. That process typically begins on a level so basic that it may, without too much inaccuracy, be termed biological: the loss is experienced as threat, and it triggers the same instinctual aggressive reactions that would occur in any other mammal exposed to a sudden assault. In terms of Jung's psychology, the archetype of the shadow—the instinctual enemy-imago that evolution has hard-wired into the human psyche—becomes temporarily constellated and projected onto any available target.

In Kübler-Ross's work with terminal patients, the anger characteristic of this phase tended to be diffuse, spilling out into any number of relationships with other human beings as well as with more abstract entities. Since an illness within the patient's own body does not usually function well as a screen on which the shadow may be projected, this is not surprising. Peak oil provides more accommodating targets for the projection of the shadow archetype, however, and so this second stage in coming to terms with peak oil very often takes the form of a quest for scapegoats—a quest that is most often directed squarely at the most powerful institutions and individuals in contemporary life. This same focus may be found all through the periphery of today's industrial societies; the insistence that the centres of wealth and influence in the modern world are essentially evil, whether sheer selfish greed or more sinister motives motivate that evil, has come to pervade much of the popular culture of the industrial world, in a shift of collective loyalties that deserves much more attention than it has received so far.

The widespread conviction that the pinnacle of the social pyramid is occupied by evil forces takes many forms in contemporary popular culture, but its manifestations in the current peak oil scene are more restricted. Here, the inner circle of wealth and influence—identified variously as the oil companies, the banking industry, the political establishment of the United States or the industrial world as a whole, or some hypothetical cabal of very rich individuals believed to control all three—is blamed for causing the peak oil crisis, by promoting the popular belief in limitless energy, by suppressing inventions that could provide limitless energy, or by inventing and promulgating the concept of peak oil as a hoax. The goal of these machinations is quite often described as a "feudal-fascist" society, a deft combination of two of modern popular culture's most negative political stereotypes, which facilitates projecting the shadow archetype onto those supposedly responsible for the end of progress.

The role of this stage in the abandonment of belief in the omnipotence of human agency is subtle, and it needs to be understood with some care. The claim that peak oil is being caused by the machinations of a malevolent elite upholds the belief that the collective human will trumps all other forces in the cosmos—after all, according to beliefs common in this stage, peak oil itself either would not be a problem, or would not be happening at all, if certain powerful people had not decided either to make it happen, allow it to happen, or pretend that it is happening. What has been abandoned is the vicarious participation of the individual in humanity's supposed omnipotence. Those in the stage of anger have begun to feel that the collective power of humanity, as represented by its rulers and institutional forms, is separate from them and, indeed, is opposed to their well-being and that of everything they value. In this withdrawal of emotional investment is the seed of the transformations that will follow.

Bargaining

With the bargaining stage, the ego takes another step towards confronting the reality of its loss, and the zone of confrontation begins to shift away from the purely instinctual reactions of the anger stage. The constellation and projection of the shadow onto some representative of the perceived threat dissolves as it becomes clear that there is no malevolent opponent causing the loss; therefore, in Jungian terms, the psyche projects any other available archetype onto the situation, seeking to redefine it in a way that will allow a relationship to be established with the threat or its source. Human beings are social primates and, like other social primates, are adept at bargaining with one another to maximize pleasure and minimize pain. These are the reactions that come into play in this stage, as the ego tries to find some way to talk the universe out of following through on the perceived threat.

In dying patients, according to Kübler-Ross's account, bargaining very often takes the form of promises of reformation. Those patients with religious convictions may promise a deity that they will conform more closely to the precepts of their faith or commit themselves to some costly or difficult religious act, such as a pilgrimage or a large donation; those without such convictions are more likely to promise their health care providers that they will stop smoking, eat a healthier diet, or conform in some other way to the precepts of current medical theory. In the case of peak oil, by contrast, this stage typically involves a collective bargain rather than an individual one: the person coming to terms with peak oil tries to find something that society as a whole can do that will mitigate the consequences of the end of cheap energy.

This may or may not involve activism on the part of the individual who is in this stage. The contemporary peak oil community is full of people who have convinced themselves that, while the age of petroleum is ending and industrial society is facing dramatic declines in energy and resources, some factor—a technology, an ideology, or some imponderable such as the human spirit—will, without any need for effort on their part, make the transition much more easy than it would otherwise be. The community also has no shortage of people for whom bargaining takes the form of part-time or full-time activism in support of some such mitigating factor. There tends to be much talk among both groups about the possibility that the coming of peak oil may turn out to be a blessing in disguise, and a range of idyllic post-peak societies have been envisioned to give such notions concrete forms.

All this is, in a sense, another round of denial, but it is denial with a difference. In the stage of bargaining, the belief in the omnipotence of human agency has broken; those passing through this stage have grasped that there are forces in the cosmos that are not subject to our species' collective will. It is a profoundly human error to personalize these forces and to go on from there to assume that they can be cajoled or bribed into compliance with human desires. Still, it is an error, and as this becomes painfully clear to the individual, the next stage begins.

Depression

With the depression stage, the ego's emotional defences fail, and it must confront the full reality of its loss. Its attempts to reject the unwelcome news, to rage at whoever is to blame, and to bargain with whoever is in control of the situation, have all gone nowhere. What remains is the hard task of integrating the loss into the ego structure—in Freudian terms, withdrawing libido from its lost object so that it can be reassigned elsewhere in the economy of the psyche; in Jungian terms, withdrawing whatever archetype has been projected onto the object so that it may either be projected elsewhere or, optimally, integrated into a more mature understanding of the self. The difficulty of this task may be measured by the title of this stage, which is not metaphorical; anything from mild to severe clinical depression may accompany this stage when it occurs in various contexts of grief.

Here, those coming to terms with peak oil have certain advantages over the subjects of Kübler-Ross's original work, who were facing their own deaths—in most cases, the most serious psychological crisis any of us will ever confront. What is being lost with the loss of belief in the myth of progress is a vision of humanity's nature and destiny that has been a powerful source of meaning in Western cultures for several centuries; it is a vision that, in the psyches of people raised in the world's industrial nations, is deeply intertwined with their sense of self, their values, and their hopes. Letting go of an influential mythic narrative of this kind is hard, but rarely as hard as coming to terms with one's own imminent death.

Still, the emotional impact of the death of the myth of progress should not be understated. Its characteristic forms in the contemporary peak oil community express a profound bitterness and rage and a sense of bereavement global in its scope. One of these forms is the claim that modern industrial society, or the human species as a whole, has failed to achieve its destiny or to live up to its potential and now must tumble back down all at once into the primitive squalor from which it so slowly emerged. Another is the claim that humanity was never destined to achieve anything worthwhile, that neurological and behavioural automatisms inherited from the prehuman past chain our species to its current self-defeating course, so that nothing better ever could have been expected of it. Another is the characterization of humanity as the "ecocidal ape", an abortion of nature, destined to drag down the whole biosphere in its own plunge into the abyss, for whom prompt extinction is the only merciful fate.

That these narratives resemble nothing so much as hostile rewritings of the myth of progress is no accident. A core part of the work of the stage of depression is finding a new narrative structure to give meaning to the ego's experience; a person who is dying must rewrite the story of his or her life in the light of its imminent ending, while one who is grieving for some other person must find a way to make his or her own story continue in the absence of one of its principal characters. In the same way, those who find themselves having to come to terms with peak oil are faced with the challenge of finding a new shape for the story of our species. It is not surprising that their first efforts in this direction tend to amount to savage parodies of the narrative they are abandoning; this allows them to get emotional distance from that narrative and also serves as a vehicle through which they can express their own bitterness, anger, and sorrow.

Acceptance

With the acceptance stage, the ego is finished coping with the emotional impact of its loss and can turn to other things. The arrival of the acceptance stage is partly determined by the completion of the various psychological tasks already described, and partly by the simple factor of time: the loss has become a familiar part of reality, and the ego, no longer fixated on the new and unwelcome experience, is able to direct more of its attention elsewhere. The transition to this stage can be gradual—a slow lifting of the depressive condition over the course of weeks or months—or sudden—an abrupt shift in affect and ideation, perhaps even comparable to a conversion experience, in which depression gives way all at once to a renewal of mental balance and a reawakening of interest in the world.

The positive features of the stage of acceptance were somewhat limited in the cases of terminal illness originally surveyed by Kübler-Ross by the simple fact that those who reached this stage rarely had long to live. In her later work (Kübler-Ross & Kessler, 2005), by contrast, the more expansive potentials of this final stage of the grieving process received more attention. Just as the outcome of a truly successful healing process is renewed health, not merely a coming to terms with being ill, the outcome of a truly successful grieving process is a renewed engagement with life and its joys, not simply an endurable compromise with sorrow and pain. This is particularly true when, as in the case of peak oil, the grief is being suffered not for the loss of one's own life or that of a person with whom one has had a close relationship, but simply for the collapse of a set of abstract beliefs about the nature of humanity and the world.

The stage of acceptance, because it involves a re-engagement with the world, differs from the earlier stages in much the same way that the diversity of life experiences differs from the relative uniformity of the human psyche's deep structure. It is thus much less simple to characterize the attitudes of those members of the peak oil community who have completed their journey through the process of grieving for the death of progress than it is to outline the attitudes of those in previous stages. A galaxy of personal factors shape the nature of each person's accommodation to the end of progress.

Age is among the most influential of these shaping factors. An elderly person who cannot expect to witness more than the opening stages of the long descent may come to terms with peak oil by deciding to take each day as it comes; a middle-aged person may set out to have some of the experiences, such as travel in foreign countries, that will likely become prohibitively expensive as the cost of transportation fuels continues to climb; a younger person may review his or her career plans and expectations, decide that the arrival of peak oil has made them irrelevant, and embark on a profession and a way of life unrelated to those he or she previously had in mind.

These are anything but hard and fast distinctions, however, and many other factors—gender, social status, ethnic and cultural background, and more—can overturn even the broadest age-based expectations. Thus, for example, there are elderly retirees in the contemporary peak oil scene whose response to the coming of a troubled future is to throw themselves into vigorous support of projects whose results they know they will not live to see, and young people who live life a day at a time in full awareness of fact that the world they know is disintegrating around them. As the reality of peak oil forces itself on the attention of a greater fraction of the industrial world's people, such complexities will become commonplace. They form one aspect of the challenge that peak oil presents to psychotherapists, and others in the helping professions, who will find themselves called upon to deal with the individual and collective psychological impacts of the arrival of a future unpleasantly different from the one most of us expect.

SIX
Facing an unwelcome future

As the industrial world moves further into the unexplored space on the far side of peak oil, and as the gap widens between the future of endless betterment predicted by the myth of progress and the future of economic contraction, social instability, and eventual technological regress that is actually taking shape around us, the conflicts sketched out in the preceding chapters trace out fault lines along which major social ruptures can be expected. At least two critical tasks await therapists, other members of the helping professions, and interested laypersons as this pattern unfolds. The first is to anticipate, at least in outline, the nature of those ruptures and their psychological impacts on vulnerable individuals—a category that, just at the moment, may include most of the population of the industrial world. The second is to prepare meaningful responses to those impacts—a task that presupposes that those who offer such responses have already come to terms with the reality of our collective situation and are not hiding behind evasions of the sort outlined in Chapter One.

Psychology as a science barely existed in the days when Southern physicians blamed "drapetomania" for the efforts of slaves to escape to freedom. It is worth recalling, however, that a great many physicians and psychiatrists in the 1950s and 1960s cooperated with the invention of "housewife syndrome", and they went along with the officially approved habit of prescribing unnecessary tranquilizers to suburban women whose experience of collective crisis was being redefined as a sign of personal inadequacy. This offers a useful lesson about how easy it can be for the helping professions to be drawn into the defence of a failing mythology, even at the expense of those they think they are helping.

As discussed earlier in this book, efforts are already under way to redefine the spread of poverty and the collapse of economic opportunity across the industrial world in purely personal terms—as a lack of appropriate education or even as a mental illness. Such efforts are likely to continue, and indeed to expand, as the economic impacts of peak oil and other forms of resource depletion spread outwards through the global economy. Thus, it is important to understand, insofar as this is possible, the shape of the future that peak oil is bringing to the industrial world.

That shape has little to do with the onward march of progress that forms the default option of the contemporary imagination of the future, and not much more in common with the apocalyptic full stop that is the one acceptable form of deviance from that orthodoxy. In all probability, rather, it resembles nothing so much as the changes the industrial world has seen during the last decade or so, extended and amplified by the continuous pressure of the same driving forces already at work in our time. As cheap and easily accessible reserves of petroleum and other fossil fuels are used up, reserves that are more expensive and difficult to access are brought on line to replace them. The additional cost is not an abstraction, or a result of market forces; it represents, rather, an increasing real cost in energy, raw materials, labour, and other resources, all of which must be continuously invested in order to keep petroleum flowing into the global economy.

Elsewhere in the economy, all other things being equal, increasing the amount of energy, raw materials, labour, and other resources that are put into a specific economic sector will increase the amount of goods and services produced by that sector. Because the increased cost of oil production in the wake of peak oil is the result of geological constraints, by contrast, this rule does not hold true for petroleum in the post-peak era. While the cost of developing new petroleum deposits and petroleum substitutes has soared, and sent the price of crude oil soaring with it, production has remained essentially flat since 2004, and no credible analysis suggests that this will change in the foreseeable future.

Thus, industrial economies are caught in a difficult bind. They can divert an ever-increasing fraction of their available resources to the task of keeping the annual production of petroleum and petroleum substitutes at something close to current levels, thus slowly starving other economic sectors of energy, raw materials, labour, and other necessities and guaranteeing economic decline by that means; alternatively, they can allow the annual production of petroleum and petroleum substitutes to decline, thus slowly starving other economic sectors of the transportation fuel on which every part of the economy depends and guaranteeing economic decline by that means. There is another, far more viable alternative—a crash programme of conservation and efficiency measures to reduce the dependence of the economy on petroleum—but embracing any such project would require a return to attitudes that were decisively rejected by large majorities of the public at the time of the Thatcher–Reagan counterrevolution, and those attitudes remain untouchable in today's political climate.

So far, the first alternative has become standard practice across the industrial world. Any project that promises to keep the world's fuel tanks topped up has been able to count on ample funding from government and private sources, no matter how small its chances of becoming economically viable and how large a burden it places on other economic sectors. The rise of the ethanol industry in the United States is a case in point.

The large-scale industrial production of fuel ethanol from corn uses more energy than the ethanol itself produces when burnt, and the economics of ethanol production are so challenging that dozens of the ethanol plants launched with such fanfare a few years ago have already gone bankrupt and shut down. Nonetheless, a US government mandate requiring gasoline blends to contain 10% ethanol has driven the diversion of 60% of the US corn crop to ethanol production. Other industries that use corn as a raw material—notably, food production—have had to contend with steeply rising corn prices and with the diversion of acreage to corn production in response to rising prices and profits; the resulting costs have been passed on to purchasers, and so the costs of expanding the US gasoline supply with ethanol have been passed on to sectors of the economy that have no direct connection to liquid fuels production at all.

RESPONSES THAT MATTER

It is by such indirect routes that the rising costs of petroleum production are loading an ever-increasing burden on the global economy. The linkages between that burden and the growing joblessness, stagnant wages, volatile markets, and shrinking government revenues that define today's economic reality are equally indirect, and so these linkages will be denied strenuously by those who have a stake in the current order of things—a category that includes, of course, nearly everyone with ready access to the political process or with influence over what appears in the mass media. Thus, it is probably safe to expect plenty of further attempts to pin blame for the impacts of peak oil on anyone and anything other than their actual cause. As this continues, what remains of the industrial world's collective capacity for rational problem solving can be expected to suffer accordingly.

The practical risks imposed on individuals by distortions of this kind are not small, for what is at stake is precisely the ability to respond to the crisis of our time in any meaningful manner. In the last few years, for example, a great many jobless persons in the United States have been encouraged by federal and state governments to get training in some new set of employment skills by enrolling in university courses and to pay for it by taking out federally guaranteed student loans, on the premise that this will bring them new and higher-paying jobs and that they will therefore have no difficulty paying off the loans. Such projects make perfect sense in terms of the myth of progress, according to which any downturn in the economy is temporary and will soon give way to a return to the rising tide of prosperity. Equally, two influential industries—the financial industry, which loans the money and then packages the loans for sale as asset-backed securities, and the higher education industry, which relies on guaranteed student loans for its survival—have had much to gain by promoting vocational re-education as the answer to joblessness.

The difficulty in all this is simply that, by and large, the new and higher-paying jobs do not exist. A great many people who have returned to college for job training have thus graduated to discover that they still cannot get jobs but now have tens or hundreds of thousands of dollars in student loan debt, which, under US law, they cannot discharge by bankruptcy. Their efforts to improve their situation by following authoritative advice, and doing what most of their peers consider to be the right thing, have substantially worsened their lot. The campaign to re-educate the unemployed is therefore a distraction rather than a solution to rising joblessness; it is a response, to be sure, but not the kind of response that matters.

Problems of this kind are all but inevitable when crisis is encountered within a collective state of mind that cannot cope with forthright acknowledgment and meaningful discussion of the nature of the crisis and the causes that are propelling it. Such a state of mind is all but universal today. Just as the followers of Dorothy Martin, the UFO believer discussed in Chapter Three, rationalized away the failure of her predictions, the followers of the civil religion of progress are rationalizing away the failure of the industrial world to continue its prophesied ascent towards a future of endless betterment. The widening gap between that imaginary trajectory and the arc of economic contraction, political dysfunction, and technological regress that defines our most likely future can be papered over for a time. During that time, any number of emotionally satisfying but counterproductive projects, such as the effort to send the jobless to college just described, will likely proliferate. The fact that they offer a convenient way to reduce cognitive dissonance, it is fair to assume, will be far more influential in the minds of most people than the fact that they do nothing to solve the problems towards which they are supposedly directed.

The theory of the double bind, also discussed in Chapter Three, offers a useful model for exploring the psychological troubles that can be expected to unfold from these misdirected projects. The first, overt and verbalized injunction, as discussed earlier, is precisely the myth of progress itself—the belief, religious in its shape and intensity, that prosperity, technological sophistication, and an assortment of other collective goods can be expected to increase over time, and that any departure from this trajectory is a temporary blip that will soon be set right. The second, covert and nonverbalized injunction is the simple fact that everyday experience no longer supports the myth of progress and will contradict it with increasing force as the industrial world continues to slide down the far side of the Hubbert curve (see Chapter One). The third injunction is the profound emotional and intellectual commitment to the civil religion of progress that pervades contemporary industrial societies, and it will make it impossible for believers in that religion to accept the concept that progress may turn out to have been a temporary phenomenon, even long after the end of progress has become an inescapable fact.

On a collective level, that double bind will likely remain in place for some time to come. The emergence of the peak oil community over the last decade and a half, though, shows that it need not remain in place on an individual level. However compelling the emotional force of the myth of progress, and however forceful a resistance the psychological mechanisms discussed earlier in this book can be expected to put up to the abandonment of that myth, many people in the industrial world have begun to ask hard questions about the shape of the future and the consequences of the collective choices industrial societies have made in the recent past. Those questions will likely become more common as the impact of peak oil on industrial economies becomes increasingly difficult to square with the expectations fostered by the civil religion of progress and as the cognitive dissonance generated by that contradiction becomes increasingly resistant to any resolution short of facing the facts.

Therapists and other members of the helping professions are likely to be among the first to notice the individual impact both of these questions and of the pressures that drive them. A person who is forced to deal with a challenge to basic assumptions about the nature and meaning of his or her life is by definition a person under significant psychological stress. The complexity of the human psyche being what it is, that stress may surface in any number of direct and indirect ways, and a good many of these are among the things that bring clients to psychotherapy, counselling, and other treatment modalities. Those who provide such modalities may find it useful, in order to offer meaningful help to clients, to be attentive to signs that the collective strains outlined in this book may be among the factors at work in any given case.

Sorting that factor out from among other sources of psychological trouble, and gauging its relative contribution to the problems faced by a client, is not likely to be a simple matter. For every client who is sufficiently aware of the cognitive dissonance between the myth of progress and the facts of everyday life to be open to a discussion of that subject, there will likely be many who remain so thoroughly entangled in the myth, and in the psychological patterns that reinforce it, that a premature attempt to bring the collective dimension into the discussion may be met with misunderstanding or outright rejection.

The situation, to return to a comparison used more than once in this book, is very much like that of a suburban housewife in the early 1960s who is depressed and dissatisfied with her life. Her own self-diagnosis, which has been shaped by the media and a constellation of cultural pressures, is that her depression and dissatisfaction are signs that something is wrong with her. It may take her therapist many sessions of careful probing to bring her to the point of recognizing that, instead, something may be wrong with her society and with the expectations about her role in life that she has internalized from family and the media.

In the same way, as the impact of peak oil whittles away at what remains of the industrial world's prosperity, a great many people will likely respond to their inability to live up to internalized economic and cultural expectations by blaming themselves or others, or in some other way using rationalizations at varied levels of complexity to explain why the myth of progress is still true even though their own life experience contradicts it. Such evasions are common enough in human psychology, and most systems of therapy have an assortment of therapeutic tools to help clients get past defensive manoeuvres of this kind. It is crucial, however, to realize that tools of this sort may turn up something other than the purely personal issues that have been the central concern of most schools of psychotherapy, and that the collective crisis defined by peak oil may be at the root of a significant number of apparently unrelated psychological problems in the years ahead.

THE FAR SIDE OF PROGRESS

That realization, however, presupposes that therapists and other members of the helping professions have themselves grappled with the reality of peak oil, its likely impacts on the future of the industrial world, and the pressures of the double bind set up by the mismatch between those impacts and the future promised by the myth of progress. Standard practice in many psychological treatment modalities requires a prospective therapist to go through a full course of therapy in the process of his or her training, so that the therapist's own psychological issues will be less likely to get in the way of the needs of clients. The same logic applies to the mass psychology of a society in crisis: those who have not yet dealt with the collective issues in their own psyches will not be well prepared to deal with them in others, and they may end up unwittingly sacrificing the best interests of their clients for the sake of a failing social mythology.

The present crisis of industrial society, as suggested above, is a particularly dangerous setting in which to take such risks. It implies no disrespect to the experience of women in the 1950s and 1960s, or the far more severe impact of slavery on African-Americans in the antebellum South, to point out that the issues excluded from the collective conversation of our time involve questions of life and death on an even greater scale than these. The combined pressures of economic contraction, environmental disruption, and resource depletion, conflicting as they do with fundamental belief systems of our time, are already placing severe strains on the collective psyche of the industrial world—stresses of a kind that could conceivably result in episodes of mass schizophrenia on the scale of the Nazi phenomenon of 1933–1945.

Millions of Germans during those years were caught by a double bind defined by the incompatibility between the cherished cultural ideology of *Deutschland über alles* and the bitter reality of defeat in the First World War. In the years ahead of us, hundreds of millions of people across the industrial world will risk falling into a comparable double bind defined by the incompatibility between an equally cherished cultural ideology of Progress *über alles* and the bitter reality of contraction and decline. In such times, as Jung pointed out in a prescient 1934 essay, the collective psychology even of the most modern and rational society can become swamped by archaic contents from the most primitive levels of the psyche, with appalling results.

It is impossible to say whether the collective psychotic break that overtook Germany in 1933 and swept across Europe in the following decade could have been prevented by some act of collective psychotherapy. It is equally impossible to say, at least for the time being, whether such a descent into delusion and mass violence is a possible future for the industrial world in the wake of peak oil, and, if so, whether that might be prevented in its turn. The points raised in this book suggest that the risk is real, and that the effort to forestall it is worth making; those same points also suggest some of the crucial elements that a response to the risk might include.

The share of that response that might reasonably be left to therapists and other members of the helping professions is, it is fair to say, a relatively limited one. One part of the work will have to be done by activists, journalists, and writers, whose central project will be that of breaking the double bind by publicly confronting the failure of the myth of progress and discussing the shape of the future defined by that failure. Another part will belong to ordinary citizens, who face the hard work of redefining their own lives in the face of a future of contraction, and who must find new sources of meaning and purpose in the emotional vacuum that the end of the civil religion of progress will leave behind. Other people and professions will have challenges of their own to face.

Nevertheless, the influence of therapists and members of the other helping professions on the shape of the future will not be small. If clients who seek help for psychological problems rooted in the collective crisis of our age are met with therapeutic approaches that redefine their troubles in purely personal terms, that envision treatment as a matter of helping the individual accept a set of largely unexamined assumptions about society and the future, or that simply medicate them into a numb acceptance of the status quo, the human cost of such measures may not be limited to the individual sphere. On the other hand, if therapists and counsellors take the presence of collective crisis into account in their work, help clients explore and articulate the cognitive dissonance they are experiencing, and provide a supportive framework in which clients can work through the stages of grief and begin the search for meaningful ways of living in a world on the far side of progress, the benefits to society as well as the individual may not be small.

Embracing this latter alternative will demand a great deal from the helping professions. As already suggested, members of those professions will have to work through the issues outlined in this book themselves. They will have to come to terms with the failure of the civil religion of progress, accept both the psychological and practical implications of a future of prolonged contraction and decline, and find their own way in a world in which the future of endless betterment promised by the myth of progress no longer provides easy answers for enduring human questions of meaning and value. They will have to re-examine the therapeutic toolkits available to them, since the difficulties posed by a crisis of the collective psyche may not necessarily respond well to methods geared to familiar personal and interpersonal problems. After all this preliminary work is done, they in turn will face both the familiar challenge of adapting the general considerations explored here to the needs of the individual client, and the potentially unfamiliar challenge of helping the client grapple with collective issues of a kind that most contemporary schools of psychology rarely address.

One of those issues—perhaps the most important of all—may be neatly defined as the rediscovery of hope. There is a mordant irony to this description: very often, those who are new to the concept of peak oil, when they do not simply dismiss the immense challenges that the end of the age of cheap energy have prepared for the modern world, complain that accepting such a view of the future is equivalent to giving up hope. Hope, they insist, comes from believing that something—some technological breakthrough, some collective awakening, or even some apocalyptic event such as the Second Coming of Christ or a landing by flying saucers on the White House lawn—will surely intervene to save us from the future that peak oil has made for us. No matter how unlikely such an event may be, they argue that trusting in its arrival is preferable to accepting that the future is what an objective assessment of the evidence suggests it will be.

Common though it is, this assertion implies a very odd definition of the concept of hope; a thought experiment that puts the same logic in a different context may help show just how odd it is. Imagine the plight of an unemployed single mother in today's America as the holidays approach. She has, like so many others in her situation, only enough money to pay the most basic expenses for herself and her children, and the clock is ticking on her unemployment benefits, which will run out after ninety-nine weeks. Her efforts to find a new job have been unsuccessful, and so it has become plain to her, as the holidays draw near, that if she is going to keep her children fed and clothed and housed, there will be no Christmas presents this year. What does she say to the children? According to the logic of the complaint just described, she presumably ought to tell them that Santa Claus will show up on Christmas Eve with a big sack full of presents for all. It is certainly true that this will fill the children with hope for the time being. It might even seem like a good idea, as long as she does not think about what will happen on Christmas morning, when eyes that had been sparkling with delight the night before look up tearfully from the bare floor to their mother's face.

Most people recognize that the right thing to do instead in a situation of that kind is to tell the truth, or as much of it as the children are old enough to grasp, and to do it early enough in the season that they can get past the inevitable misery and set to work on making the best of things. Oral histories of the last Great Depression contain any number of stories of this kind—the holiday decorations pieced together from wrappers and scraps, the depressingly plain meal livened up with a few little touches or sheer make-believe, the little doll made from rags and burlap sacking that remains a treasured possession three quarters of a century later, and so on. If hope is to be had in such a difficult situation, it is going to come by that route, not by making gaudy promises that are not going to be fulfilled.

However, that sort of ethical and psychological clarity requires a willingness to confront the realities of a difficult situation without evasion, which is something that is in very short supply just now. All the many obstacles discussed in the earlier chapters of this book—the prestige of the myth of progress, the tangled historical processes that have made that myth the central narrative of a widely and passionately believed civil religion in our time, the psychology of previous investment and the dangerously irrational drives that feed into it, the cultural forces that have defined disbelief in progress as deviant behaviour, and the understandable desire of people faced with the prospect of loss to put off the hard work of dealing with that loss as long as possible—raise barriers in the way of the necessary but difficult step of coming to terms with a future that is not the one that most people in the industrial world have been raised to expect. All these factors are normal behaviours of the human psyche. In ordinary times, they provide a stabilizing influence on the collective thinking of a culture or an age; it is simply our misfortune that these are not ordinary times.

FROM HUBRIS TO HOPE

The psychological factors just listed, however, should not be confused with hope. The meaning of that word "hope" is a vexed question just now, and not only because the US President in office as of this writing used the word to get into office in

2008 via one of the most cynical political campaigns of modern times. Even before it got stripped of its remaining content by the Obama campaign's marketing team, the old virtue of hope had become tangled up in the modern culture of entitlement and been twisted completely out of shape in the service of marketing disguised as cheap sentimentality. "When you wish upon a star, / Makes no difference who you are, / Anything your heart desires / Will come to you . . ." Readers of a certain generation will recall hearing that bit of doggerel out of the mouth of an animated insect. Relying on that principle in the real world is a bad idea at the best of times; in the conditions faced by the industrial world at the end of the age of cheap energy, it may well prove lethal.

Such manoeuvres have tended to obscure the important differences between the concept of hope and the facile optimism of the privileged, the sort of thinking that convinces so many people nowadays that nothing really unpleasant can happen to them. A great many people thus think that being hopeful in the face of peak oil means assuming, against all the evidence, that some ample replacement will be found in time to allow the industrial world to keep its current energy-intensive lifestyles in existence into the indefinite future. An even larger number of people think that a hopeful approach to the limits to growth means trying to convince themselves that those limits don't apply to them, or that there will turn out to be some way for them to evade the limits, or that somebody or other will bail them out before their refusal to deal with the limits lands them with consequences harsher than they want to think about.

It is interesting, by contrast, to consider the historical conditions that surrounded the evolution of the concept of hope in the ethical thought of the Western world. Like so much of post-classical Western culture, that concept emerged out of the creative collision between Greek philosophy and Christian religious ideas in the late-Roman world. That was not an age of economic expansion and rising standards of living. Quite the contrary: as the Roman Empire ran up against its own limits to growth, and then drove itself into bankruptcy and collapse trying to defend borders defined in a more expansive age, economic crises and a soaring tax burden sent standards of living steadily downwards while the Empire lasted. Its fall, in turn, brought an age of chaos in which whole regions that had once known widespread literacy, busy market economies, and such amenities as central heating devolved into fragmented, impoverished, and drastically underpopulated successor states in which eking out a bare subsistence was an achievement that not everyone managed (Ward-Perkins, 2005).

The ideas concerning hope that are common in modern popular culture would not have lasted long in the protracted downward spiral of the Roman world. The concept of hope as an ethical virtue, by contrast, became universally accepted throughout the Western world during that same downward spiral. This happened because hope is not optimism. It is not the passive expectation that good things will inevitably come one's way. Rather, it is the recognition that no matter what the circumstances might be, there are positive goals that can be achieved if they are pursued with forethought and a sustained willingness to try (Snyder, 1994).

Compare hope to any of the other character traits celebrated in that harsh time, and the distinction is even clearer. Courage, for example, is not a facile assurance that one is destined to win. It is the combination of personality traits that makes it possible to do the right thing in the face of danger and fear. This is, among other things, the opposite of the conviction that victory is inevitable. That is a matter of simple logic—someone who recognizes no danger and feels no fear is not courageous no matter how many risks he unknowingly runs—but it also has practical dimensions. One of the commonplaces of military history, for example, is the army that believes too deeply in its own invincibility and so collapses in panic when the battle turns against it, because it has never had to grapple with the possibility of defeat.

In the same way, hope does not depend on a sense of entitlement that insists the universe is obligated to provide us with whatever happy ending we think we want. In any real sense, hope is incompatible with notions of that kind. Hope is the combination of personality traits that responds to difficult circumstances by finding some good that can be achieved, and then strives to achieve it. The capacity to hope is thus, among other things, a crucial source of meaning in circumstances where more ordinary conceptions of meaning have failed (Frankl, 1959).

The common contemporary sense of entitlement, in turn, is precisely equivalent to the belief in the inevitability of victory, and it produces the same sort of brittleness as that discussed above. Just as an army convinced of its invincibility can panic and fail catastrophically when a battle goes against it, a sense of entitlement very often gives way to despair when its expectations are frustrated, and it is despair, ultimately, that feeds the refusal to face realities that so often disguises itself as hope in contemporary culture.

It is for this reason, for example, that apocalyptic fantasies always flourish in the aftermath of grandiose movements for social and spiritual transformation (Greer, 2011b). The three primary apocalyptic currents in contemporary American culture as of this writing are cases in point. The New Age movement's recent obsession with the claim that the Mayan calendar predicted the end of the world on 21 December 2012 is simply one expression of a broader current of millenarian belief, which has fixated on many previous dates and will doubtless find new dates in the future. Behind it lies the failure of the earlier New Age conviction that a minority of awakened minds could create their own reality and usher in a new era of peace, love, and enlightenment, without the benefit of global cataclysms or alien landings (Ferguson, 1980).

In the same way, the current evangelical Christian obsession with the supposed imminence of the Rapture marks the bitter endpoint of a trajectory that began with the buoyant optimism of the "Jesus freaks" and the Good News Bible, when enthusiastic young Christians recruited from the 1960s counterculture convinced themselves that they could remake the world in Christ's image. The trajectory of the environmental movement from the hopeful days of the 1970s to the climate change apocalypticism of today is another example of the same arc.

All three of these movements, in other words, are tracing out the rise and fall of Dorothy Martin's circle of UFO believers on a grander scale. In the process, hubris disguised as one kind of hope has given way to despair disguised as another kind of hope, and the concept of hope itself risks being discredited. That is profoundly unfortunate, because it is when grandiose narratives crash to the ground that hope, in the sense of the word outlined above, becomes a psychological necessity.

That necessity will become ever more difficult to escape in the years ahead of us. Behind the rise and fall of the environmental, New Age, and Christian fundamentalist movements stands the vaster rise and fall of another attempt to build Utopia here on Earth, the attempt we call industrial civilization. Today, as the limits to growth tighten around the industrial world like a noose and an economy geared to perpetual expansion shudders and cracks in the throes of decline, among the things that are needed most is the willingness, in a time of gathering darkness, to locate what lamps can still be found, and to light them. To return to the metaphor offered earlier, it is time to listen to the voice that tells us, "Honey, I'm really sorry, but Santa Claus isn't coming this year". Having heard that, and done whatever grieving we need to do, we need to draw in a deep breath, accept the hard facts of our future, and make the best of the limited options the choices of the past have given us. That process could be greatly facilitated by therapists and other members of the helping professions who have come to terms with the realities of the present age and done their own grieving for the imaginary future promised by the myth of progress, and who are thereby able to help others navigate the same transition from hubris to hope.

REFERENCES

Bateson, G. (1955a). A theory of play and fantasy. In: *Approaches to the Study of Human Personality* (pp. 39–51). Psychiatric Research Reports No. 2. Arlington, VA: American Psychiatric Association.

Bateson, G. (1955b). *Epidemiology of a Schizophrenia.* Paper presented to a conference on The Epidemiology of Mental Health, Brighton, Utah (May). In: *Steps to an Ecology of Mind* (pp. 194–200). New York: Chandler, 1972.

Bateson, G. (1960). The group dynamics of schizophrenia. In: L. Applebee, J. Scher, & J. Cumming (Eds.), *Chronic Schizophrenia: Explorations in Theory and Treatment* (pp. 90–105). London: Collier-Macmillan.

Bateson, G., Jackson, D., Haley, J., & Weakland, J. (1956). Toward a theory of schizophrenia. *Behavioral Science, 1* (4): 251–264.

Bayles, M. (1994). The shock-art fallacy. *Atlantic Monthly, 273* (2): 18–20.

Bellah, R. (1967). Civil religion in America. *Journal of the American Academy of Arts and Sciences, 96*: 1–21.

Ben-Yehuda, N. (1985). *Deviance and Moral Boundaries.* Chicago: University of Chicago Press.

Boortz, N. (2007). *Somebody's Gotta Say It.* New York: William Morrow.

References

Boyer, P. (1992). *When Time Shall Be No More: Prophecy Belief in Modern American Culture*. Cambridge, MA: Harvard University Press.

Bywater, I. (Trans.) (1952). *Aristotle: Poetics*. Chicago: William Benton.

Callenbach, E. (1975). *Ecotopia*. San Francisco, CA: Banyan Tree.

Campbell, C. (2004). *The Coming Oil Crisis*. London: Multi-Science.

Campbell, C., & Laherrère, J. (1998). The end of cheap oil. *Scientific American, 278*: 78–83.

Churchill, W. (1956). *The Birth of Britain*. New York: Dodd, Mead & Co.

Coser, L. (1962). Some functions of deviant behavior and normative flexibility. *American Journal of Sociology, 68*: 172–181.

Deffeyes, K. (2005). *Beyond Oil: The View from Hubbert's Peak*. New York: Hill and Wang.

DeJean, J. (1997). *Ancients against Moderns*. Chicago: University of Chicago Press.

deMoll, L. (Ed.) (1977). *Rainbook: Resources for Appropriate Technology*. New York: Schocken.

Dentler, R., & Erikson, K. (1959). The function of deviance in groups. *Social Problems, 7*: 99–107.

Douglas, J. (1977). Shame and deceit in creative deviance. In: E. Sagarin (Ed.), *Deviance and Social Change* (pp. 59–86). Beverly Hills, CA: Sage.

Duncan, R. (1993). The life-expectancy of industrial civilization: The decline to global equilibrium. *Population and Environment, 14*: 325–357.

Ehrlich, P., Ehrlich, A., & Holdren, J. (1977). *Ecoscience: Population, Resources, Environment*. San Francisco, CA: W. H. Freeman.

Ferguson, M. (1980). *The Aquarian Conspiracy*. New York: Tarcher.

Festinger, L. (1957). *A Theory of Cognitive Dissonance*. Stanford, CA: Stanford University Press.

Festinger, L., Riecken, H., & Schachter, S. (1956). *When Prophecy Fails*. Minneapolis, MN: University of Minnesota Press.

Frankl, V. (1959). *Man's Search for Meaning*. Boston, MA: Beacon Press.

Freud, S. (1912–13). *Totem and Taboo. Standard Edition*, 13.

Freud, S. (1917). Mourning and melancholia. *Standard Edition, 14*: 237–258.

Freud, S. (1921). *Group Psychology and the Analysis of the Ego. Standard Edition*, 18.

Friedan, B. (1963). *The Feminine Mystique*. New York: W. W. Norton.

Goode, J., & Ben-Yehuda, N. (2009). *Moral Panics: The Social Construction of Deviance*. Oxford: Wiley-Blackwell.

Greer, J. (2008). *The Long Descent: A User's Guide to the End of the Industrial Age*. Gabriola Island, BC: New Society.

Greer, J. (2011a). *The Wealth of Nature: Economics as if Survival Mattered*. Gabriola Island, BC: New Society.

Greer, J. (2011b). *Apocalypse Not*. San Francisco, CA: Viva Editions.

Hadot, P. (1998). *The Inner Citadel*. Cambridge, MA: Harvard University Press.

Hanegraaff, W. (1996). *New Age Religion and Western Culture*. Boston, MA: Brill.

Heinberg, R. (2003). *The Party's Over: Oil, War, and the Fate of Industrial Societies*. Gabriola Island, BC: New Society.

Hirsch, R., Bezdek, R., & Wendling, R. (2005). *Peaking of World Oil Production: Impacts, Mitigation, and Risk Management*. Washington, DC: United States Department of Energy.

Hubbert, M. (1956). *Nuclear Energy and the Fossil Fuels*. Houston, TX: Shell Development Company.

Hubbert, M. (1974). *U.S. Energy Resources: A Review as of 1972*. Washington, DC: Senate Committee on Interior and Insular Affairs.

Jacobi, J. (1959). *Complex/Archetype/Symbol in the Psychology of C.G. Jung*, trans. R. Manheim. Princeton, NJ: Princeton University Press.

James, W. (1890). *The Principles of Psychology*. New York: Henry Holt.

Johnson, W. (1978). *Muddling toward Frugality*. Boston, MA: Shambhala.

Jung, C. (1934). Wotan. In: *Civilization in Transition* (pp. 179–193), trans. R. Hull. New York: Pantheon, 1964.

References

Jung, C. (1968). Archetypes of the collective unconscious. In: *The Archetypes and the Collective Unconscious* (pp. 3–41). Princeton, NJ: Princeton University Press.

Jung, E., & von Franz, M. (1972). *The Grail Legend.* London: Hodder.

Knox, R., & Inkster, J. (1968). Postdecision dissonance at post time. *Journal of Personality and Social Psychology, 8* (4): 319–323.

Konigsberg, R. (2011). *The Truth About Grief.* New York: Simon & Schuster.

Kübler-Ross, E. (1969). *On Death and Dying.* New York: Macmillan.

Kübler-Ross, E., & Kessler, D. (2005). *On Grief and Grieving.* New York: Scribner.

Kunstler, J. (1993). *The Geography of Nowhere.* New York: Free Press.

Kunstler, J. (2005). *The Long Emergency.* New York: Atlantic Monthly Press.

Lamy, P. (1998). *Millennium Rage.* New York: Plenum.

Lemert, E. (1951). *Social Pathology.* New York: McGraw-Hill.

Maciejewski, P., Zhang, B., Block, S., & Prigerson, H. (2007). An empirical examination of the stage theory of grief. *Journal of the American Medical Association, 297* (7): 716–723.

Matza, D. (1969). *Becoming Deviant.* Englewood Cliffs, NJ: Prentice-Hall.

May, R. (1991). *The Cry for Myth.* New York: W. W. Norton.

McClenon, J. (1984). *Deviant Science: The Case of Parapsychology.* Philadelphia, PA: University of Pennsylvania Press.

Meadows, D. H., Meadows, D. L, Randers, J., & Behrens, W. (1972). *The Limits to Growth.* New York: Universe.

Mills, C. W. (1943). The professional ideology of social pathologists. *American Journal of Sociology, 49*: 165–180.

Mills, C. W. (1951). *White Collar: The American Middle Classes.* Oxford: Oxford University Press.

Minuchin, S. (1974). *Families and Family Therapy.* Cambridge, MA: Harvard University Press.

Muller, M. (1882). *Introduction to the Science of Religion.* London: Longmans, Green.

Nisbet, R. (1980). *A History of the Idea of Progress.* New York: Basic Books.

Nye, D. (1996). *American Technological Sublime.* Cambridge, MA: MIT Press.

Nyhan, B., & Reifler, J. (2010). When corrections fail: The persistence of political misperceptions. *Political Behavior, 32* (2): 302–330.

Perera, S. (1986). *The Scapegoat Complex: Toward a Mythology of Shadow and Guilt.* Toronto: Inner City.

Ponting, C. (1992). *A Green History of the World: The Environment and the Collapse of Great Civilizations.* New York: St. Martin's.

Ramage, J. (1997). *Energy: A Guidebook* (rev. edition). London: Oxford University Press.

Roszak, T. (1972). *Where the Wasteland Ends.* Garden City, NY: Doubleday.

Rue, L. (1989). *Amythia: Crisis in the Natural History of Western Culture.* Tuscaloosa, AL: University of Alabama Press.

Russell, J. (1991). *Inventing the Flat Earth.* New York: Praeger.

Sagan, C. (1980). *Cosmos.* New York: Random House.

Savinar, M. (2004). *The Oil Age Is Over.* Sebastopol, CA: Savinar.

Schultz, R., & Alderman, D. (1974). Clinical research and the stages of dying. *Omega, 5* (2).

Schumacher, E. (1973). *Small Is Beautiful: Economics as if People Mattered.* New York: Harper.

Seife, C. (2008). *Sun in a Bottle: The Strange History of Fusion and the Science of Wishful Thinking.* New York: Penguin.

Shils, E. (1975). *Center and Periphery: Essays in Macro-Sociology.* Chicago: University of Chicago Press.

Snyder, C. (1994). *The Psychology of Hope.* New York: Free Press.

Tainter, J. (1988). *The Collapse of Complex Societies.* Cambridge: Cambridge University Press.

References

Thorndyke, L. (1949). *The Sphere of Sacrobosco and Its Commentators.* Chicago: University of Chicago Press.

Tobin, K. (2002). The reduction of urban vulnerability: Revisiting 1950s American suburbanization as civil defence. *Cold War History, 2* (2): 1–32.

Todd, J., & Todd, N. (1980). *Tomorrow Is Our Permanent Address.* New York: HarperCollins.

Ward-Perkins, B. (2005). *The Fall of Rome and the End of Civilization.* Oxford: Oxford University Press.

Weatherhead, P. (1979). Do savannah sparrows commit the Concorde fallacy? *Behavioral Psychology and Sociobiology, 5* (4): 373–381.

INDEX

Index